EAST EUROPEAN MONOGRAPHS, NO. VII

VIENNA BROADCASTS TO SLOVAKIA

1938-1939
A CASE STUDY IN SUBVERSION

HENRY DELFINER

EAST EUROPEAN QUARTERLY, BOULDER
DISTRIBUTED BY COLUMBIA UNIVERSITY PRESS,
NEW YORK AND LONDON

1974

Copyright © 1974 East European Quarterly
Library of Congress Catalog Card Number 73-94175
ISBN 0-914710-00-1

Printed in the United States of America

contents

ii

The author wishes to express his deep sense of gratitude to Dr. Ruhl J. Bartlett of the Fletcher School of Law and Diplomacy for his many helpful suggestions, to Dr. Arthur Hruby of Vienna, Austria, for his invaluable work of translating the voluminous Slovak source material into German, to Dr. Joerg K. Hoensch of the University of Tuebingen for his friendship, help and advice based on an unparalleled mastery of the subject, and to Dr. Yeshayahu Jelinek of the Hebrew University, Haifa, for his painstaking examination of the manuscript and the many insights his comments afforded the author.

INTRODUCTION

The subject of the Vienna broadcasts to Slovakia during the crucial months between the Munich Agreement and the fall of Czecho- slovakia in March 1939 has been largely neglected or at best treated as a footnote to the history of that period. My interest in it was aroused by the conviction that the extended German propaganda, campaign conducted at that time to win over the Slovaks to the German side was bound to have had an important influence on events. Further investigation of the broadcasts has convinced me that a study of the campaign is worthwhile for several reasons. It sheds additional light on the history of the Munich era by showing the erosive effects of prolonged psychological warfare on national morale. It further shows new uses of anti-Semitism as part of the German psychological warfare effort to drive a wedge between Czechs and Slovaks which proved a potent factor in the subversion of Slovakia.

It is an indication of the lack of attention which the broadcasts have received that most writers refer solely to the climactic days of the radio war in March 1939 while neglecting the fact that the Slovak language series had gone on for almost six months before culminating in the much publicized March broadcasts. There were probably as many as 170 Slovak language broadcasts from Vienna in the time between September 1938 and March 1939. Most of them must be considered lost except for fifty-one which have been located and reassembled in this volume. The most important source by far are two books of Ludovit Mutnansky the writer and announcer of the Vienna Slovak series between September 1938 and August 1939. Other sources were the large number of German documents that have been preserved in the German archives and in the National Archives in Washington, D. C. The fifty-one broadcasts printed in this volume, while representing about a quarter of the total, very likely include those that are the most significant. The reason for this assumption is that Mutnansky was bound to select the broadcast scripts for filing in the German archives. It is thus safe to assume the probability that the broadcasts included in this volume are representative of the total as regards importance of content.

While an effort has been made to represent the broadcasts as complete entities, there has been an elimination of news concerning countries other than Slovakia, which was frequently included in the original broadcasts but has no direct bearing on this study. Regarding translation, the rule that I have tried to observe has been to keep it as literal as possible and to deviate from that rule only where absolutely necessary in order to convey to the reader an emotional impact not brought out by a literal version of the original.

Slovak place names and the names of Slovak individuals have been spelled in the Slovak way with the sole exception that diacritical marks have been eliminated to simplify the printing process.

In referring to the time of day the twenty- four hour system is used to improve clarity.

CHAPTER I

THE PURPOSE OF THE BROADCASTS

While it is not the purpose of this book to draw a detailed picture of German policy toward Czechoslovakia and toward Slovakia, a brief summary of policy may be useful as an introduction to what follows.

GERMAN POLICY TOWARD CZECHOSLOVAKIA AFTER MUNICH

German policy toward Czechoslovakia in 1938 and 1939 can best be described by the word *zerschlagen* (dismember) used in Hitler's directives of November 10, 1937, and May 30, 1939. There was, however, a brief period of thaw in Germany's hard line immediately following the Munich Agreement. Prompted by the belief that the Czechoslovak government would now cooperate wholeheartedly with Berlin, one wing of German policymakers, the dominant wing, seemed to favor some degree of cooperation. This was a very short-lived experiment, however, and by the end of 1938 the original aim of destroying the Czechoslovak state became once again official policy.

Speculation as to the reasons for this reversal of policy turns mostly around two factors. The first was Hitler's gnawing suspicion that the "Benes spirit" might reawaken in Czechoslovakia. It is often held that the frequent German reference to the Benes spirit was merely a propaganda device designed to make the Czechs more pliable. But there can be no doubt about Hitler's genuine hatred for Benes, about the fact that democratic influences in Czechoslovakia, which were considered by the Germans to be part and parcel of the Benes spirit, persisted after the Munich Agreement, nor about the additional fact that Benes was very much alive in exile and was bound to exercise some direct or indirect influence over the lives of his countrymen, even though he realized the extremely dangerous position in which his country found itself and avoided any action that would embarrass his successors. It is safe to conclude, therefore, that even though Hitler's original hatred for Benes was dormant for a while immediately following Munich, it did not take much to reawaken it, thus causing German policy to relapse into the anti-Czech convulsions that preceded the Munich period.

The second reason for the change in policy was purely strategic and seems to have revolved around military and industrial considerations. The military in Germany were very much aware of the usefulness of Czechoslovakia in any moves to the east, and the industrial planners headed by Hermann Goering[1] believed that Slovakia in particular was rich in many raw materials that Germany needed. Both the military and the industrial leadership of Germany thus had a   special interest in Czechoslovakia, and this interest was generally directed toward taking complete control of all or part of the country.

It seems clear that by the end of 1938 the suspicions about a revival of the Benes spirit and strategic considerations combined to gain ascendancy over the thaw policy that had culminated sometime in November 1938 in the drafting of a treaty between Czechoslovakia and Germany by the staff of the German Foreign Ministry which, however, was never acted upon.[2] Under the terms of that treaty Czechoslovakia would have become an outwardly independent country under German tutelage as Slovakia was to become later.

The beginning of 1939 thus marked renewed hostility toward Czechoslovakia, and this hostility did not end until Czechoslovakia was dismembered in March 1939.

GERMAN POLICY TOWARD SLOVAKIA

Parallel to the two policies toward Czechoslovakia as a whole, there were also two prominent lines of German policy regarding Slovakia immediately following the Munich Agreement. One line favored Slovak independence; its chief advocate was Hermann Goering. It is known that Goering received Slovak separatist leaders in October 1938[3] and agreed with them that independence was the answer to the Slovak problem. During a second meeting on November 11, 1938,[4] Goering had to modify his original statement somewhat by saying that while independence was the ultimate solution, Slovakia would have to work as an autonomous unit of Czechoslovakia for the time being. A few days after this second meeting Goering was told by Foreign Minister Ribbentrop that Hitler did not wish any further negotiations with the Slovak separatists.[5] As long as German relations with the new Czechoslovak government were friendly, the backers of Slovak independence, led by Goering, were effectively kept under control by Hitler himself and by Ribbentrop who probably believed at the time that Germany might gain complete control over the Prague government without the need to split Czechoslovakia asunder.

However, after the beginning of 1939 and the return to a hard German position toward the Prague government, Hitler received the leading Slovak separatist Tuka in February 1939; in effect he apologized for having mistakenly believed that Slovakia wished to rejoin Hungary and for not having realized that she wanted to be independent. In other words, the German realization that Prague was not likely to become sufficiently pliable to allow Germany to rule all of Czechoslovakia through a strong pro-German central regime automatically meant that Slovak independence had now become official German policy. Hitler told Tuka that Slovakia would suffer badly if she remained on the side of the Czechs. Goering met again with Slovak separatist leaders, led by Dr. Ferdinand Durcansky, at the end of February 1939[7] and also indicated clearly that Slovakia could not expect German support unless she broke away from Prague. The German plan that emerged by 1939 was now to use Slovak secession as the excuse for taking over the Czech western part of the country by claiming that the country had never been viable and, left to itself, would represent a threat to world peace.

GERMAN PROPAGANDA POLICY

In a supplement to the German plans for Operation Green, the code word for the assault on Czechoslovakia, issued on May 30, 1938, the propaganda aspect of the operation was defined by Hitler as follows:

> Propaganda warfare must on the one hand intimidate the Czechs by means of threats and wear down their power of resistance; and on the other hand it must give the national racial groups indications as to how to support our military operations and influence the neutrals in our favor. Further instructions and determination of the appropriate moment are reserved to me.[8]

As time went on this plan had to be adjusted to changing circumstances particularly with regard to its Slovak aspects which fell within the realm of national racial group operations referred to in the master plan. Nonetheless the basic outline never lost its validity as a modern example of the classical "divide and conquer" model which the Germans executed with considerable skill and success.

Although the plan applied, strictly speaking, only to military psychological warfare operations, it probably corresponded to overall propaganda policy. The emphasis on wearing down the enemy's power of resistance, at the time referred to as "war of nerves," proved to be one of its most effective elements.

THE GERMAN PROPAGANDA LINE TOWARD SLOVAKIA

In line with overall German policy of seeking the destruction of the Czechoslovak state, no effort was spared by Hitler in the pre-Munich crisis to lure the non-Czechs of Czechoslovakia away from the Czechs and to urge them to side with the German minority in that country in taking a stand against the Prague government. The following excerpts from one of Hitler's best known speeches of that period show the arguments he used to achieve this goal. The speech was made at the Berlin Sportpalast on September 26, 1938, and contained the following passages regarding Slovakia:

> The Western statesmen at Versailles could have established the fact that there is no such thing as a Czechoslovak nation but only Czechs and Slovaks and that the Slovaks did not wish to have anything to do with the Czechs but (applause drowns out the rest). So in the end through Mr. Benes these Czechs annexed Slovakia. . .
>
> He demands of the Slovaks that they should support aims to which the Slovak people are completely indifferent. For the Slovak people wish to have peace - and not adventures.[9]

Small wonder that the Slovak separatists welcomed the above speech so passionately. Hitler had in effect told the Slovaks that he was willing to treat them quite differently from the hated Czechs and had suggested to them that they had nothing in common with the Czechs. By pursuing a policy of friendship with Germany the Slovaks could have peace, while any backing of the Czechs was likely to involve them in war and defeat.

A detailed analysis of the above passage shows that German propaganda toward Slovakia could be based on the following elements:

- Czechs and Slovaks have nothing in common.
- Czechs pursue adventurist policies likely to lead to war and ruin.
- Slovaks by pursuing an independent, pro-German policy can preserve peace and prosperity for themselves.
- German friendship and protection is Slovakia's for the asking.
- Slovaks are the victims of the Czechs.

To these basic ingredients of German propaganda toward Slovakia must be added a few highly effective "hate" elements, particularly anti-Semitism and anti-Bolshevism, which rounded out the basic appeals set forth by Hitler in the Sportpalast speech.

Looking back to the atmosphere of fear that pervaded Europe at the time of the Munich crisis, the propaganda appeal launched by Hitler had much to make it highly attractive to the Slovaks, and it is to the great credit of the vast majority of that people that their basic loyalty to the idea of a Czechoslovak state was strong enough to prevent a wholesale desertion by Slovaks of the endangered nation. It was only after several months of incessant propaganda and threats that the Slovak nation unenthusiastically went the way Berlin had by then determined she should go.

ORIGIN OF THE BROADCAST IDEA

As has been seen, German policy regarding Czechoslovakia based on dismemberment was interrupted in late 1938 by a brief thaw induced by German hopes of gaining complete domination through a Czechoslovak puppet regime. Both dismemberment or complete domination from within required a vigorous propaganda effort which started immediately upon the annexation of Austria. The Austrian capital had been closely involved in Czech affairs for centuries prior to 1918, and there were many individuals in Austria who by background, experience, or political interest were particularly well-suited for directing the political and propagandistic penetration of Czechoslovakia that was set in motion by March 1938.

The first written evidence that a Czech language radio program was being planned as part of the propaganda offensive is found in a letter of Arthur Seyss-Inquart, the Reichsstatthalter (governor) of Austria, to Foreign Minister Ribbentrop on June 22, 1938, in which he mentions that a suggestion had been made to him[10] some time earlier to include a Czech language program on the Vienna radio. He had not had any further news on the subject and asked Ribbentrop for his instructions. It is significant that the men to whom Seyss-Inquart refers as having relayed the original suggestion to him were connected with the Volksdeutsche Mittelstelle (VdM), the German central organization of German minorities abroad which played a highly important role in German subversion activities in Czechoslovakia and elsewhere.

The files do not show what Ribbentrop's answer to Seyss- Inquart was, but it is known that Dr. Wolfgang Muehlberger, the propaganda expert who was later placed in charge of Southeast European broadcasting, was approached sometime in August 1938 by Karl Hermann Frank or by Wilhelm Sebekovsky, two of the ranking officials of the SdP, the National Socialist- oriented German minority party in Czechoslovakia, with a view to taking over these broadcasts. The broadcasts actually started on September 3, 1938, and were at first under the office of Joseph Buerckel, the Nazi Gauleiter of Austria. At the end of October 1938 they were transferred from Buerckel's control to that of the Reichsstatthalter Seyss-Inquart.[11]

Seyss-Inquart played one of the leading roles in the German penetration of Slovakia. Born in the Sudeten-German area of Czechoslovakia he was entrusted by Hitler with the task of informing him on conditions in Slovakia. He did this with the help of two trusted colleagues, Dr. Franz Hammerschmid and Dr. Fritz Flor.[12] Hammerschmid soon became what might be called the coordinator of Slovak information and was Seyss-Inquart's right-hand man in the German subversion of Slovakia.

PURPOSE OF THE BROADCASTS

At the time the control over the broadcasts was transferred from Buerckel to Seyss-Inquart in October 1938, Dr. Muehlberger wrote a detailed report on the accomplishments of the program during the first few weeks of operation which coincided with the Munich crisis. Part of the report was devoted to a concise statement of the propagandistic purposes of the broadcasts emphasizing the following points:

> To shake the confidence of the Czech people in its government.
> To shake Czech confidence in their supposed Allies.
> To expose Bolshevism as an enemy of the people and as a threat to European peace.
> To stress the positive aspects of German peace policy.
> To show the economic and social folly of an arms race.
> To mobilize the will for self-determination among minorities living in Czechoslovakia.
> To emphasize German domestic achievements.
> To stress German economic strength and the advantages to Southeastern Europe of economic contacts with Germany.[13]

It is obvious that this list represents a propagandistic corollary to Hitler's plan of smashing the Czechoslovak state. Dr. Muehlberger later confirmed that the overall propaganda aim at the time was the *Dekomposition* (dismemberment) of Czechoslovakia.[14] The brief post-Munich alternative of allowing Czechoslovakia to remain intact as a German puppet state never found much favor among the Vienna-based propagandists. During the period of the thaw the Vienna programs continued to pursue a slightly subdued disintegration policy. When, however, at the beginning of 1939 disintegration became official policy again, the broadcasts pursued this objective more vigorously than ever.

ORGANIZATION OF THE BROADCASTS

The methods used by the German government in organizing the broadcasts are of importance in two respects: for one they show how much priority was given to this aspect of the total propaganda effort, for another they indicate whether and to what extent the German government was willing to publicize its interference in the affairs of another country.

The degree of priority given to the broadcasts is illustrated by the fact that the Vienna station, one of the larger units of the German state broadcasting network, devoted prime time to it on a daily basis for an extended period. For the first few weeks the Slovak language program was scheduled every evening at 1930 hours which, in Central Europe, is dinner time. By November 1938 it was shifted to the equally important lunch period, and remained there until at least the end of 1939. The new time was 1310 hours and the length of the broadcasts was usually from 1310 to 1315 hours. The time from 1300 to 1315 hours was (and still is) a traditional news period; thus the final five minutes of that period were devoted to broadcasts in the Slovak language which, of course, caused quite a bit of grumbling among local Viennese listeners most of whom did not understand a word of what was said and may not have been aware of the purpose of the broadcasts.

As for the question of German willingness to concede publicly its interference in Czechoslovak internal affairs, especially after the conclusion of the Munich Agreement, this is answered by the fact that the broadcasts were made part of the regular program of the Vienna station[15] and were normally listed in the official radio programs printed in all the newspapers. When the broadcasts began, an attempt was made to explain them by saying that the Czech minority in Vienna had requested the programs because they could not depend on the news from their home country, but no one took that explanation seriously, and the fact that there was no further reference to it after the initial announcement indicates that the German government apparently did not feel the need to supply an excuse for the activity. Having seen during the Munich crisis that the allies of Czechoslovakia were not willing to risk war on her behalf, they quite rightly assumed that those allies would scarcely risk German displeasure by objecting to the broadcasts. As will be shown later, the lack of notice the broadcasts received in the Western capitals is in itself remarkable and indicates the degree to which the appeasement policy toward Germany had at that time become accepted among the Western European nations.

At first the program was given the name *Pravda Vitezi* (The Truth Will Win), also the official motto of the Czechoslovak Republic. This name seems later to have been used for the Czech broadcasts exclusively, however. The Slovak broadcasts, which started two weeks after the Czech program, had the following introductory statement of their own: "This is Radio Vienna. Here is the news in Slovak language. The motto of new Slovakia is: To turn back is impossible: we must march forward."[16] This introduction seems to have preceded every single broadcast at least until well into 1939.

In addition to the split into a Czech and a Slovak program which came abot by the middle of September, there were also separate broadcasts in Ukrainian, the language spoken in the easternmost province of Czechoslovakia, Ruthenia (or Carpatho-Ukraine). The names of some of the announcers are known. The Slovak announcer Ludovit Mutnansky has already been mentioned. He was succeeded in August 1939 by an ethnic German by the name of Rosskopf. The Czech announcer during the initial period was a teacher named Musil, while the Ukrainian announcer was a Mr. Bacinsky.[17] In connection with the Ukrainian language programs it might be added that Ukrainian was also spoken by several million Ukrainians then living in eastern Poland and, of course, by the Ukrainians of the Soviet Union. The Ukrainian language broadcasts were thus intended for an audience far greater than that of Ruthenia. Their strategic purpose is clear in view of the rapidly deteriorating relations between Germany and Poland after the collapse of Czechoslovakia.

It seems that the broadcasts in the three languages spoken in Czechoslovakia continued uninterruptedly until the end of 1939 when a break occurred. Muehlberger left and joined the German legation in Slovakia as press attache. Mutnansky had already ended his broadcasting activity in August 1939. Sporadic Slovak language broadcasts continued well into the war years, but the regular daily programs of the period of 1938-1939 were not resumed. The reason for this is easy to surmise; the Slovak government had by then become so thoroughly subservient to German wishes that it was apparently not deemed necessary to duplicate the Slovaks' own propaganda efforts through German stations.

[1]It must be kept in mind, however, that Goering was also in charge of the German air force and that air bases in Slovakia were therefore an additional factor of great interest to him. (See also *Documents on German Foreign Policy,* no. 68.)

[2]See Joerg K. Hoensch, *Die Slowakei und Hitlers Ostpolitik,* p. 215, footnote 32.

[3]*Documents on German Foreign Policy,* no. 68.

[4]Ibid., no. 112.

[5]*Documents on German Foreign Policy,* no. 120. This was on November 17, 1938. Two days later, Ribbentrop instructed Seyss- Inquart not to "activate" Tuka. See Chapter IV.

[6]*Documents on German Foreign Policy,* no. 168. Vojtech Tuka soon became one of the most prominent men in post-Munich Slovakia, and from 1939 to 1944 he was prime minister of Slovakia. He represented the extreme right-wing of the Slovak People's Party and was also known for his strongly pro-German views.

[7]*Documents on German Foreign Policy,* no. 184.

[8]Francis L. Loewendeim, *Peace or Appeasement?* (Boston: Houghton Mifflin Co., 1965), p. 15.

[9]Norman H. Baynes, *The Speeches of Adolf Hitler,* vol. II (London: Oxford

[10]They were Dr. Franz Wehofsich of the VdM and SS Obergruppenfuehrer Lorenz, at that time in change of German participation in international organizations. Letter of June 22, 1938 in Handakten Seyss-Inquart, Bundesarchiv, Coblenz.

[11]Information given to the writer by Dr. Muehlberger in July 1969.

[12]Seyss-Inquart's deposition during the Nuremberg trials, see *Trial of the Major War Criminals,* vol. XV, p. 637.

[13]Wolfgang Muehlberger, *Arbeits-und Organisationsbericht ueber die tschechischen, slowakischen und ukrainischen Relationen des Reichssenders Wien. In Handakten Seyss-Inquart.*

[14]Information given to the writer by Dr. W. Muehlberger in July 1969.

[15]The broadcasts were made on a wavelength of 506.8 meters, a regular broadcasting frequency; in other words, these were not shortwave broadcasts.

[16]Frantisek Vnuk states that these words were followed by the motto "A new Slovakia without the Jews," and he further states that the broadcasts ended with the following sentences: "Slovaks do not forget the Jew was, is, and will be the greatest enemy of the Slovak nation and of the Slovak state. Therefore, with Sidor against the Jews." Frantisek Vnuk, "Slovakia's Six Eventful Months October 1938-March 1939," *Slovak Studies,* vol. 4 (1964), p. 96. The fact that Mutnansky does not record the final sentences in his books is most likely accounted for by the fact that Sidor became almost a "non-person" after March 1939.

CHAPTER II

PROPAGANDA CONTENTS AND PERSONALITIES

CONTENTS OF RADIO PROPAGANDA

A brief listing of the most important elements making up the propaganda appeal of the Slovak broadcasts would include the following.

Self-pity. Reference has been made earlier to Hitler's remark that the Slovaks had been annexed by the Czechs. This was the opening needed for a campaign of self-pity. Whether self-pity happened to be a dominant characteristic of Slovaks is hard to say; it would be conceivable as a result of their long history of foreign domination. Examples of the approach used in the broadcasts can be found in the numerous references to the poor, hard-working, honest Slovak who is perpetually abused and deprived by foreign masters of what is rightfully his.

It is known that humiliation by foreign powers is a usual and powerful source of nationalism. Since humiliation and self-pity are closely related emotions it is easy to see why this would be an important element in building Slovak nationalism as well as hate for those foreigners who were accused of being guilty for the Slovak suffering. Anti-Semitism and anti-clericalism will be discussed under a separate heading.

Anti-Czech Propaganda. This was a rather touchy area in view of the close relationship between the two nations and their joint history during the twenty years after World War I. It was handled in three ways. First, Czech policies were associated with Judaeo-Bolshevism or Freemasonry thus clouding the real issue and "contaminating" the Czech image in the minds of the Slovak listeners. Second, during the period immediately preceding Slovak independence accounts were given of alleged Czech hostility to Slovakia to arouse anti-Czech feelings. Examples of this are found in the broadcast of January 7, 1939. It is also reflected in Durcansky's speech of March 10, 1939, when he accused Prague of undermining Slovak financial strength. Closely related were earlier references to Czech exploitation of Slovakia such as that in the broadcast of October 30, 1938. Finally, reports of Czech troop movements such as those mentioned by the broadcasts of March 4 and March 7, 1939, were also undoubtedly designed to exacerbate Czech-Slovak tension.

Anti-Marxism. Curiously enough this is a subject on which Mutnansky, the author of the broadcasts, has least to say, possibly because of his own strong anti-capitalist leanings which are particularly evident in his anti-Semitic tirades. His predilection for the term "revolution" and his occasional praise for socialism are further indications that Mutnansky's attitudes were in this respect more leftist than those of orthodox National Socialists. Nevertheless he did his share by linking, as was then customary, Jews to Bolshevism, thus extending the opprobrium reserved for the Jews to the Bolsheviks.

Anti-Masonic Propaganda. The opposition of National Socialism to the Masonic movement is well known. It seems that Mutnansky made particularly frequent use of it because he could indulge his anti-Semitism by linking the two groups. There was another aspect that made "Mason-baiting" a useful pastime for Mutnansky. The opposition to Freemasonry was one idea which Nazism and Catholicism shared. For this reason it was quite advisable for someone like Mutnansky who tried to "sell" National Socialism to a predominantly Catholic group to use a slogan which he knew was backed by their church.

Racism. This subject is covered rather explicitly in Muehlberger's instructions for the broadcasts beginning with that of November 20, 1938. The broadcast of November 22, 1938 shows its prompt implementation. Further evidence of it will be seen in the broadcast of January 1, 1939, and in others where racial measures to solve the Jewish question are held to be the only correct ones.

Special appeal to the workers. It is a fact of some significance that throughout the broadcasts a definite effort was being made to win over Slovak workers to the side of the propagandists. If Slovakia had been a highly industrialized nation this would scarcely require comment, but the fact that Slovakia was a highly agricultural nation would make one expect that special appeals, if any were to be made, would be primarily directed to the farmers. Several reasons may account for this. It may have simply been a reflection of Mutnansky's own leanings toward the working class. This could scarcely have influenced a series of broadcasts, however, whose general policy was set by German officials.

This leaves two other possibilities. One is that Slovak workers may have been assumed to favor National Socialism, and the other that they may have been felt to offer a particularly suitable target for National-Socialist indoctrination, possibly because the hold the Church had on them was weaker than that on farmers. In the author's opinion it is the latter of these arguments that comes closest to the reasons for the special effort made by the broadcaster to win over the Slovak worker. In addition, the depression may have affected Slovak workers even more than farmers so that the social reforms frequently mentioned in the broadcasts were a need and a promise holding special importance to the working class. Examples of special concern with workers will be found among others in the broadcasts of December 4 and December 11, 1938.

Anti-Panslavism. The fact that a German radio station was inciting a Slavic nation, the Slovaks, against its close Slavic brothers the Czechs, while at the same time preaching to them the importance of race, nationalism, etc., seems highly incongruous, and many of the listeners may have felt this. For this reason there was a strong need to neutralize such sentiment, and this was done by telling the Slovaks that they actually were closely related by blood to the German race, while they were not closely related at all to the Czechs. The authority on which this handy discovery was based was the race expert Ernst Wagner.[2] It seems, however, that such obvious maneuvering with "scientific" data did not suffice to dislodge the feeling of racial or national consanguinity the Slovaks held for the Czechs or for the Russians. As a result, several broadcasts attacked Panslavism, one of these being the broadcast of February 28, 1939.

Pro-German Propaganda. This will be found throughout the series being a fairly obvious content of all the broadcasts. However, it may be worthwhile to mention a few outstanding examples, such as the Durcansky broadcast of March 10, 1939, with its famous closing appeal to the Slovak nation to fight for national freedom "with the help of our friends, the great German nation," or the equally well-known reference in Karol Murgas's speech of March 13, 1939, to "the great savior of National Europe, Adolf Hitler" holding his protecting hand over Slovakia. A very early example, which is not contained in the collection of broadcsts below but is reliably reported to have been broadcast on November 18, 1938,[3] stated that "the German Reich is watching the struggle of the Slovak people for realization of its autonomy with understanding and with rising interest. The Slovaks as nation and as state possess the full sympathy of the Reich." For an expression of similar sentiments see also the broadcast of October 30, 1938.

Fear. One of the strongest weapons in any propaganda campaign is the use of fear. This weapon was included in the German radio propaganda campaign to Slovakia though in a muted form. On several occasions the somewhat ominous statement was made that "political developments in Europe have not yet ended." meaning that German expansion had just begun.[4] Tuka, one of the Slovaks politically closest to the Vienna propagandists, compares the effect of the Vienna broadcasts to that of "Big Bertha," the famous World War I German artillery piece that shelled Paris from a great distance.[5] The choice of the simile here cannot have been altogether accidental, and undoubtedly the effect of some of the broadcasts, especially where they involved personal ostracism and invective, must have been such to cause fear. It is certain that this was part of their purpose since waging a war of nerves was part of Hitler's basic propaganda guideline.

Other instances where fear, or extreme uneasiness, can be shown to have resulted from the broadcasts are reported by Sidor whose remarkable resistance to German pressure in March 1939 marks him as a man of much stronger than average nerves.[6] Nevertheless, he too makes this revealing statement about the effects of a few days as Premier of Slovakia under constant German harassment: ". . .after the crude facts of four nights and four days my organism

is starting to experience nervousness. Radio Vienna launched its torpedo attacks against my person, knowing full well that if I left the command post the
nation would resemble an alarmed herd."[7]

Still another indication of the use of fear in German propaganda methods
can be found in the memoirs of Viliam Kovar, an ardent backer of Durcansky's separatist right wing. Speaking of his brief address on Radio Vienna
during the "radio war" days, he explains why he did not attack anyone personally: "I felt that the situation in Bratislava had again become tense due to
the recent speeches on Radio Vienna. This being so why should one name any
individuals thus provoking ill-considered action?"[8]

These few indications will suffice to show that throughout the series, and especially during the climactic days of the radio war, the broadcasts contributed
to the creation of that highly nervous situation that preceded surrender in
Slovakia and elsewhere.

SPECIAL BUILD-UP CAMPAIGN

It must be emphasized that in addition to the general propaganda line
followed by the Vienna broadcasts there were also specific campaigns conducted at various times to build up Slovak statesmen who enjoyed German
backing.

The first Slovak statesman singled out for such special treatment was Vojtech Tuka, and indeed it would seem that he was the only major Slovak figure
who had complete and constant German support, not only in the period under
study but throughout the remaining years of Slovak independence. It will suffice to point out a few broadcasts showing the strong support Tuka received
from Radio Vienna - the programs of September 26, October 24, November
24, December 1, and December 9, 1938. They are typical of the attempt to raise
Tuka to the status of national martyr and national hero.

Another Slovak statesman who enjoyed the Vienna radio's backing for a
time was Ferdinand Durcansky. Chapter VIII contains his well-known broadcasts of March 10 and March 12, 1939. It seems, however, that there were
earlier broadcasts heaping praise on Durcansky. While no texts are available of
any such earlier broadcasts, their existence is known from a report of the
British consul in Bratislava, Peter Pares, dated February 3, 1939, which includes the following statement:

> The only Radical Ministers at present are Dr. Durcansky and
> Sidor. The former has rather lost prestige on account of his misuse
> of the Slovak broadcasts from Vienna as a means of advertising
> himself and his brother, who are both lawyers. It is only recently

that the broadcasts have been made to serve this purpose. They were originally devoted to anti-Czech propaganda.[9]

It may be merely accidental that Mutnansky's earlier book makes no reference to these broadcasts mentioned by Pares. It is far easier to determine why his second book makes no mention of Durcansky whatsoever. Durcansky fell from German favor in 1940, and Mutnansky was involved in his ouster as will be seen. He now had every reason to avoid pointing to Durcansky's contribution to Slovak independence. This explains why Mutnansky's earlier book, published in 1939 when Durcansky was still in power, includes Durcansky's March 10 radio speech under his name and photograph, while Mutnansky's second book, published in 1942, includes the same speech but omits mention of the speaker's name or photograph.[10]

The third personality to enjoy a build-up on Radio Vienna was Karol Sidor. The broadcasts of January 3 and January 6, 1939 illustrate this well. Also one of the dispatches to the Foreign Office by the British minister in Prague, Sir Basil Newton, dated as early as November 1, 1938, states "Deputy Sidor, for example, who though not a member of the government is being backed by the German wireless to replace Dr. Tiso as Prime Minister. . ."[11] indicating that Sidor enjoyed the support of Radio Vienna as early as the end of October 1938. In Sidor's case support was to be of even shorter duration than in that of Durcansky and was to shift from lavish praise to calumny within a few weeks.[12]

ANTI-SEMITISM

The Importance of Anti-Semitism in the Slovak Broadcasts

The broadcasts do not necessarily make attractive reading. Some of them are brimful with hate, but the emotional impact of these messages on the listener is lost unless they are read in their entirety. The hate mongering is particularly evident in the anti- Semitic broadcasts whose importance in this series went far beyond indulging Mutnansky's personal hatreds, real enough though they were.

Anti-Semitism supplied the cement that was to bind the Slovak listener to the German propagandist to whom he had neither national nor even ideological links, since the average Slovak was a devoutly religious Catholic, while the typical fanatical Nazi was a man whose only gods were the Fuehrer and the German nation. Such cement was needed particularly because this was one of the first instances where Germans propagandized non-Germans, and the choice was fortuitous from the German point of view as there is no doubt that anti-Semitism was a prevalent feeling in Slovakia.[13]

Once the propagandist had formed this link to the listener he went on to exploit it in order to create dissension between Czechs and Slovaks. Using existing feelings against Jews to his advantage he went on to identify Czechs with Jews thus transferring anti-Jewish feelings to the Czechs. Once this identification had been established it was emphasized by repetition until many, if not most, listeners were bound to accept it to some degree. If the listeners were convinced anti-Semites this was probably enough to turn them into convinced anti-Czechs. If they were less inclined to base their thoughts and actions on blind hate, they were nevertheless likely to develop a certain caution in espousing or voicing any pro-Czech sentiments. The result was that by clever manipulation of an existing dislike for Jews the propagandist succeeded at first in alienating and then in dividing Slovaks and Czechs. Having accomplished this he had achieved a major objective.

The use of anti-Semitism in the German propaganda campaign contains many important lessons. Utmost of these is the fact that the   propaganda served as a means of dividing Czechs and Slovaks in order to achieve a German objective, namely the dismemberment of Czechoslovakia. This lesson of employing hatred to serve against the best interests of a people by dividing them from their friends is one that has not lost its relevance. It demonstrates vividly how disaffection can lead to disunity and from there to apathy, defeatism, and defeat.

Mutnansky's Anti-Semitism

In speaking of broadcasts over a German station in the Nazi era it may well appear that any special reference to anti-Semitic content is superfluous since that is to be expected. It must be said in explanation for this special reference, however, that Mutnansky's brand of anti-Semitism was of an intensity that went beyond the usual, even at the time and place in question. It can perhaps be likened to the case of Ukrainian collaborators of the Germans during World War II who often exceeded the savagery of their masters.

Thus it is not surprising that in several cases comments by German officials about Mutnansky stressed his anti-Semitism. The most interesting example of this is a letter written in August 1939 by SS Obersturmfuehrer Dr. Chlan of the Vienna SD office in which he defends Mutnansky against those who, in compliance with the Slovak government's wishes, had terminated his services. Chlan mentions specifically that Mutnansky's broadcasts enjoyed wide popularity "particularly because of their anti-Semitic tendency.[14] An almost identical comment was made by Mutnansky's former superior, Dr. Muehlberger, who called Mutnansky's anti-Semitic broadcasts successful because they fell on fertile ground in Slovakia.[15] Muehlberger mentioned the same fact, although more obliquely, in a report written in February 1939 in which he lists anti-

Semitic content in the broadcasts as eliciting particular response from Slovak
listeners.[16] As for the reasons for this hatred, it will be seen that Mutnansky
claimed that the Jews had ruined his parents. Perhaps to this should be added
the known fact of his earlier dismissal for theft from Piestany, the large Slovak
spa which at that time was reported owned or managed by a Jewish family.

One of the foremost experts on Nazi propaganda stresses the importance of
anti-Semitic content in Nazi propaganda in Slovakia when he states:

> Indeed, the exaggerated claims Hitler made for the propaganda
> value of antisemitism nearly held true in Eastern Europe. Here, an-
> tisemitism proved a disintegrating and demoralizing force; it ac-
> companied the corrosion of the political system that had been es-
> tablished by the peace treaties, and it accelerated this process . . . In
> addition, it appealed to those politicians who were either dis-
> satisfied with the post-war settlement, or who were oversensitive to
> the stresses it had generated; this was particularly true of Slovakia.[17]

It is also important to stress in this context that the Tiso government, while
by no means philo-Semitic, proceded more slowly and deliberately in taking
anti-Jewish measures than the German government deemed desirable. Mutnansky was naturally in the forefront of those urging the Slovak government to
take stronger and more decisive action and may even have been an influence in
German needling of the Slovak government. Much of the early dislike between
the German Nazis and the Tiso government was due to this difference of approach to the Jewish question. Tiso's dislike of Mutnansky was thus also at
least partly connected with Mutnansky's radical anti-Semitism.

Note on Mutnansky's Talmudic Quotations

A few more words may be in order about the numerous Talmudic
quotations used by Mutnansky to fire his listeners' hatred against the Jews:

These quotations are taken verbatim from religious hate literature,
specifically from Johann Andreas Eisenmenger, a German Talmud critic who
lived at the turn of the seventeenth and eighteenth century, and from Dr.
Justus (Aron Briman), a nineteenth century German critic of the Jewish Code
of Laws, the Shulchan Aruch. However, instead of quoting his source as being
Eisenmenger, Justus, or some other author, Mutnansky refers the reader to the
Talmudic or other original source of the Eisenmenger or Justus passages he
quotes, thus implying that it is identical to the original source whose number
and verse he cites. In other words, Mutnansky quotes verbatim what highly
biased critics have to say of an original text using as his reference the original

passage cited by the critic and disregarding completely the fact that the original text may, and indeed does, vary widely from the quotation.

In one important case he quotes an alleged Jewish source authorizing the killing of heathens using an obviously wrong reference (Chosen 285).

It is easy to excuse Mutnansky's ignorance of scientific rules on proper quotations, but it is something quite different to find an excuse for his proliferation of hate literature without paying any attention to the truthfulness of its content.

One of the highly important points involved in the difference between some of the quotations from religious hate literature used by Mutnansky and the originals revolves around the question of whether the words used to describe non-Jews refer exclusively to heathens or can be interpreted to include Christians. Mutnansky cannot have been conversant with the fact that the Talmud was written between 200 and 500 A.D. in a largely non-Christian part of the world and that even the later Shulchan Aruch was largely the work of Joseph Caro, a Jew who lived in Moslem countries at the turn of the fifteenth and sixteenth century.

As for the harshness of some original quotations concerning the heathen, it must be kept in mind that religious tolerance is a product of the last two centuries and has by no means become universal even today. Consequently, criticism leveled against "ancient" men, some of whom lived almost two thousand years ago and none of whom lived much later than the end of the Middle Ages, should actually apply with even greater severity to those "modern" men who kindle the flames of hate with writings dating from times when intolerance was almost universal and who distort those writings to boot.

For the benefit of readers who are interested in the details of this subject a comparison of Mutnansky's text with those of his mentors has been supplied showing beyond any doubt the origin of some of his quotations. One of his quotations, to which unfortunately no reference can be made, is *La Silva Curiosa*. The author has been unable to locate it and believes it to be the product of an earlier author of Eisenmenger's leanings.

The identity between Mutnansky's passages and those of his anti-Semitic mentors will be evident from the following pages which will show Mutnansky's texts, the anti-Semitic literature, on which they are based, and the Jewish original texts to which the distorted texts refer.

Mutnansky's text:

Ludovit Mutnansky, *Tu rissky vysielac Vieden,* (Vienna: Julius Lichtner, 1939), p. 18.

"You must kill even the most honest of the heathen." (Avoda Sara 26.2)

Taken from:
Johann Andreas Eisenmenger, *Entdecktes Judenthum,* (Koenigsberg. 1711), vol.
II, p. 215.

> "The Talmudic tractate Sopherim states: Thou shalt kill even the
> most honest of the heathen. And this is also found in the tractate
> Avoda Sara 26.2 in the first line of the Tosephoth."

Original version:
Babylonian Talmud, Hebrew edition, Vol: Avoda Sara (Jerusalem: El
Hamekorot Ltd., 1958-63), p. 52. Tosephot (comments) on Avoda Sara 26.2.

> "But if you say that when we have said in the Tractate Sopherim,
> Chapter XV, that the best of the Canaanites is condemned, one
> must say that in the Tractate Kiddushin of the Jerusalem Talmud it
> is said that this is in time of war. . ."

It must be noted in connection with this Talmudic source for Eisenmenger's
contention that the emphsasis of the commentator is clearly to point out that
the rule stated in the quotation from Sopherim applies to the time of war. This
weakened Eisenmenger's argument considerably, and to offset this he maintained that (a) the Jews had eliminated the harsher references from the Tractate
Sopherim in the Amsterdam edition of the Talmud and (b) that they had in-
serted the milder reference from the Tractate Kiddushin of the Jerusalem
Talmud to avoid criticism. In other words, where the sources were not to his
liking he suggested that they had been tampered with.
    It will also be noted that even in the harsher Tractate the target is clearly
identified as Canaanites, eliminating all doubt that the reference applied
specifically to pagans.

Mutnansky's text:

Mutnansky, *Tu rissky vysielac Vieden,* p. 21.

"Every Jew who passes a ruined Church is obligated to say: Praised be the
Lord who has destroyed this house of idols. When passing a Church that is
standing he must say: Praised be the Lord who extends his anger against
criminals. When he sees 600,000 Jews he must say: Praised be the Lord full of
wisdom. But when he sees Christians he must say: Your mother will be exposed
to shame and delivered to derision."
(Orach Chajim 224.2)

Taken from:

Dr. Justus (Aron Briman), *Judenspiegel,* quoted in Jakob Ecker, *Der "Judenspiegel,"* pp. 34, 35.

> "Law 9: Every Jew is obligated when passing a Church (of Christians) that has collapsed to say: Praised be the Lord who has destroyed this house of idol worship, and when a Jew passes a Church (of Christians) that is still standing he is to say: Praised be the Lord who extends his anger for criminals, and when he sees 600,000 Jews together he is to say: Praised be the wise Lord; but when he sees AKUM (Christians), he is to say: Your Mother is full of shame and she who has born you has become an object of derision."

Original version:
Shulchan Aruch, Orach Chajim 224.2.

> "Whoever sees a place where idol worship has been eradicated within theLand of Israel is to say: Praised be Thou O Lord, our God, King of the Universe, who has eradicated idol worship from our Land; if it is outside of the Land, he is to say: . . .who hast eradicated idol worship from this place! In both cases he is to continue: As Thou hast eradicated it from this place, mayest Thou eradicate it from all places,and turn back the heart of their worshippers to Thy service."

Shulchan Aruch, Orach Chajim 224.5

> "Whoever sees 600,000 Israelites in one place is to say: Praised be Thou O Lord, our God, King of the Universe, who understandest hidden matters; if the gathering is made up of heathens. however, he is to say: Your mother will be put to shame, she who has born you will blush with shame; behold the end of the heathen is the desert, drought and solitude."

A brief glimpse will suffice to see that the prevailing spirit in these original passages is not the hatred evident from Dr. Justus's Law 9, but love of God and a steadfast opposition to idolatry that is melancholy rather than hateful. The text of the blessing is based on Jeremiah 50.12.

Mutnansky's text:
Mutnansky, *Tu rissky vysielac Vieden,* p. 22.

> "God perjured himself when He said that the Jews who had wandered through the desert had no claim to the life to come. Later

He regretted his oath and did not keep it. Again when He brought about the reconciliation between Abraham and Sarah He even lied and that is why it is permissible to lie for the sake of peace and of conciliation." (Baba Mezia 87.l)

Taken from:
Eisenmenger. *Entdecktes Judenthum,* vol. I. pp. 4l, 42.

"Furthermore Rabbi Eliezer imputes perjury to God in the Talmudic tractate Sanhedrin ll0.2 where he says: . . .Rabbi Eliezer thus concludes that God swore that the Jews who wandered in the desert were to have no part of the future life, later however regretted the oath and did not desire to keep it. Ninth they teach that God hid the truth and lied in order to maintain peace and unity between Abraham and Sarah. . . From this our wise men conclude that it is permissible to lie for the sake of peace. This is taken from the Talmudic tractate Baba Mezia 87.l as can be seen in the text and in Rabbi Solomon's interpretation."

Original version:
Der Babylonische Talmud, German edition. Lazarus Goldschmidt, ed., vol. VII (Berlin: S. Calvary & Co., 1903), p. 498, on Sanhedrin ll0.2.

"The generation that wandered through the desert has no share in the world to come etc. The Rabbis taught: The generation that wandered through the desert have no share in the world to come because it says (in the Bible): In this desert they shall be consumed and here they shall die; (the word) consumed (refers to) this world, here they shall die (refers to) the world to come. Furthermore it is said: And I swore in my wrath; They shall not come to my resting place - words of Rabbi Akiba. Rabbi Eliezer said: They will have a share of the world to come, because it is said: Assemble my faithful ones, those who joined my Covenant at the altar of sacrifice. How can I then explain (the words) and swore in my wrath? - I swore in my wrath but I withdrew from it."

The leniency of Rabbi Eliezer's argument about Numbers 14.35, that even the sinful generation of the desert should not be assumed to have been cut off from the world to come, is the important element of this passage. From this follows his further argument to the effect that God had sworn in his wrath and would therefore reconsider this action once his wrath had subsided. While Eisenmenger could have attacked this argument for its anthropomorphism, it certainly does not show the lack of love or respect for God to which

Eisenmenger points. It is one thing to call God a perjurer as Eisenmenger claims the Talmud here does, and it is something quite different to say that God is not above revoking a harsh decree once his anger has been appeased. *Der Babylonische Talmud,* German edition, Vol, VI, pp. 787- 788, on Baba Mezia 87.l.

> "It is said: And my Lord is old, and it is said; and I am old, the Holy One blessed be He, therefore did not repeat what she had said? - The school of Rabbi Ishmael taught as follows: Peace is so important that even the Holy One, blessed be He, changed a word for its sake as follows: and Sarah laughed in her heart etc. and my Lord is old which is followed by: And the Lord spoke to Abraham etc. and I am old."

The point of this rather involved passage about Genesis 18:12, 13, is the following: Sarah having been told by the three angels that she is to have a child doubts that this is possible in her advanced age and explains that she and her husband are too old. When the Bible later mentions God telling Abraham of Sarah's words it merely refers to God mentioning the first part of Sarah's statement to the effect that she was too old, from which the Rabbis gathered that God did not wish to cause disunity between Abraham and Sarah by repeating her full words to him since they might hurt his feelings. Again Eisenmenger concludes from this that the Talmud calls God a liar while the whole emphasis of the text is on a very noble thought, namely on the importance of preserving peace to which the idea of God omitting part of an account for its sake is entirely subordinate. It is one thing to call God a liar, as Eisenmenger claims the Talmud here does, and it is something quite different to say that God is not above omitting part of an account to maintain peace.

ANTI-CLERICALISM

Another element of the Slovak broadcasts is a careful but steady note of anti-clericalism. Mention has already been made of Muehlberger's program for the broadcasts beginning with November 20, 1938. It included not only the emphasis on racism but also on anti-clericalism. His instructions read as follows:

> (We want) "a series dealing with the topic of political Catholicism and its dangers for the nation. This series is to be prepared with utmost tact. The treatment of this difficult topic is of importance at this moment because the Slovak clergy maintains its anti-German attitude and takes no action to remove old prejudices against Germany."[20]

On the other hand it must also be realized that the Nazi party of 1938 and 1939 had left its earlier outward courtesy toward the church generally, and toward the Catholic church in particular, far behind. The annexation of predominantly Catholic Austria had been followed by a fairly open anti-clerical campaign by the Nazi Party in that country. The purpose of this campaign was to teach the clergy to keep out of politics or, putting it differently, to remain silent on any issue where religious doctrine and Nazi ideology clashed. It is against this background of a Nazi ideology that had become openly hostile to, even contemptuous of, Catholic opposition to its own excesses that the atmosphere prevailing in Germany at the time of the broadcasts must be studied, it being clear to the German propagandists that Slovakia was, if anything, even more solidly Catholic than Austria. One of the first issues on which Slovakian Catholicism and Nazi ideology clashed concerned treatment of the Jews. There was at the time a fairly widespread movement in Slovakia for Jews to convert to the Christian faith. This movement apparently was welcomed by considerable parts of the Catholic clergy who viewed it as a purely religious affair. In Nazi eyes, however, the attitude of the clergy represented interference in what was seen as a purely racial matter subject only to state and not to clerical action. Reference has already been made to the acrimony caused by this clash of attitudes and how this affected the position of Mutnansky.

The anti-clerical tone of some of the broadcasts will sometimes consist of hints and at other times of omissions. Examples of the hints can be found wherever the question of Jewish conversions comes up, and the broadcasts indicate (wherever) that the only acceptable solution to the problem is a racial one. Another such case is the reference to the need for improving Slovak social conditions and that this has nothing to do with religion.[22] In other instances, criticism is made of the church for doing nothing for the care of the children of the poor. The omissions are somewhat harder to locate, but they are of equal, if not deeper, significance. For one it will be noted that the word Christian, though used with great regularity, is not used as a religious term, but as an ethnic expression. Other instances include the ending "peace to those of strong will" in the broadcasts at Christmas time, the eulogy to Hitler in the broadcast of December 24, 1938, and so forth.

How close this anti-clerical note is to Mutnansky's own convictions and to those of his friend Vavra can be seen from a letter written by both men on October 19, 1938, when the impending transfer of the broadcasts from Buerckel's control to that of Seyss-Inquart may have inspired doubts about their future. They say: "The Slovak Minority in Vienna has always been and is friendly to National Socialism but it still frequently finds itself under the leadership of clerically minded men whose influence can be totally eliminated through the broadcasts." Speaking of Slovakia they go on: "What has been said of the Slovak minority (in Vienna) goes doubly for the situation in Slovakia proper. The Slovak clergy is fairly strongly anti- National Socialist. The people is (sic) being influenced in that sense from the pulpits. The Vienna broadcasts are the means of countering this by enlightening the people with National Socialist ideology."[24]

How closely these anti-clerical views were shared by Muehlberger himself can be seen from his report of February 1939, in which he comments on the Tiso group in the Slovak government which was solidly backed by the Catholic clergy:

> The weakest point of Tiso's group is that he is formerly and actually responsible for all activity of the Slovak People's Party and that almost none of the many promises made since October 6, 1938 have so far been kept. This affords an opportunity to launch a campaign against the harmful influence of the Vatican since people are starting to realize that the Catholic clergy is not everywhere defending the true interests of the people. Examples of this are the Jewish question, the solution to the social problems, etc.[25]

PERSONALITIES

Ludovit Mutnansky - Biographical Data

The man who more than anyone else has become associated with the Slovak broadcasts from Vienna is Ludovit Mutnansky. His two books are the source for most of the broadcast texts that have been survived, and he was the author of all the regular broadcasts between September 15, 1938, when he started his activity, and the beginning of August 1939, when he had to leave his position with Radio Vienna.

Mutnansky's political views were strongly anti-Czech and in favor of Slovak separatism. He was vehemently pro-German and indeed should be looked upon as a Slovak in German service rather than as the persecuted Slovak patriot seeking and being given refuge in Germany - as that he like to portray himself.

A further outstanding trait was his pathological anti-Semitism, a result of sad experiences his parents allegedly had in business dealings with Jews which, Mutnansky claimed, ruined them. A far from harmonious domestic life with frequent wife-beating episodes gives a further insight into the man's character,[26] with its marked inclination toward self-pity - something which Mutnansky may have transferred from his person to his nation.

Born in Bratislavia in 1904,[27] he was, prior to 1932, in charge of athlectics in the spa of Piestany where he was also secretary of the local soccer club. Taking advantage of his latter position he embezzled club funds and as a result was dismissed. He was then made sports editor for *Slovak*, the organ of Hlinka's People's Party, and became at the same time a minor official of that party.

Again he embezzled funds, this time membership dues of the People's Party, was fired, and disappeared from Bratislava.[28] It is not at all clear from the record what Mutnansky did between 1934, when he was fired from his second job, and 1938 when he started his work for the German government, except that he was in Germany at the time of the Olympic Games of 1936 about which he wrote a book showing his pro-Nazi inclinations. In his autobiographical introduction to his books Mutnansky gives the impression that he had been working at the People's Party office in Bratislava up until September 1938 and that it was Hitler's speech at the Nuremberg rally, coupled with the Czechoslovak mobilization, that made him decide to go to Germany where the leader of the (Nazi) Slovaks in Vienna, Rudolf Vavra, helped him to get his position on the Vienna Radio. Mutnansky's appointment received the approval of the counter-intelligence section of Goebbels's propaganda ministry.[29]

While Mutnansky's autobiography is supported by at least one recent Slovak book which mentions that he was sent to Vienna in September 1938 by Ferdinand Durcansky, there is a conflict between this information and the fact that he was fired and disappeared in 1934. Still another source, this one in the same political camp as Mutnansky, states that he left Czechoslovakia following the Tuka trial in 1929.[31]

As will be seen, Mutnansky made a number of important and powerful enemies during his broadcasting career including some leading officials of the independent Slovak state. This may account for the fact that the Slovak government in August 1939 asked Mutnansky's superiors in Vienna for his removal and that the Germans obliged. Mutnansky, who had taken charge of organizing the Hlinka Guards' Foreign Legion in September 1938, remained in charge of that organization until September 1940, while simultaneously serving as social attache of the Slovak legation in Berlin. His bitterness toward the Slovakian government led to a period of active scheming with other pro-German Slovaks who felt they had been pushed aside. The head of this group apparently was Tuka[32] and his active lieutenants were Mutnansky, Rudolf Striezenec, a journalist, and Karol Murgas. In the early part of 1940 this group was active in sending appeals to the German government asking for a complete takeover of Slovakia by Germany as a protectorate. One of their main obstacles was Foreign Minister Durcansky whose original pro- German attitude had given way to one of rigorous support for genuine Slovak independence. The pro-German group therefore concentrated its efforts on obtaining Durcansky's ouster and brought about a meeting between Hitler and the Slovak leadership on July 28, 1940, at Salzburg. Tiso protested this flagrant German interference in Slovak affairs but had to give in to Hitler's demands. Tuka thereupon became foreign minister, and Mach, another member of the pro-German group, became minister of interior.

By 1942 Mutnansky was back in Bratislava where he wrote the second of his books which was followed by some other writings later in the war. In

Seyss-Inquart.

st of November 22, 1938.

of the SD-Leitabschnitt Vienna, Microfilm T-175, serial 514, roll 514, National
ington D.C.

f January 1 and January 9, 1939.

oreward to Mutnansky's books.

ication of Sidor's strong nerves can be seen in the broadcast of January 6, 1939,
article in *Slovak* praising Sidor's calm during the Munich crisis.

Ako Vzniko "Slovensky Stat" (Bratislava: Vydalo Politicke Literatury, 1958), p.

tizen aus den Maerztagen 1939," p. 27.

on *British Foreign Policy*, 3rd series, vol. IV, no. 97 (London: His Majesty's
e, 1950-51).

e to Mutnansky's books in broadcast of March 10, 1939.

on *British Foreign Policy*, vol. III, no. 245.

' broadcast of March 13, 1939. Refer also to Chapter I, footnote 16.

s opposed to racial, anti-Semitism had been part of the political plank of the Slovak
since its very beginning.

of the SD-Leitabschnitt Vienna.

given the author by Dr. Muehlberger, July 1969.

Muehlberger, *Zur politischen Entwicklung in der Slowakei*, Microfilm T-120, serial
frame 442384, National Archives, Washington D.C..

an, *Nazi Propaganda*, (London::Oxford University Press, 1964), p. 82.

pparently to Choshen Hamishpat, one of the parts of the Shulchan Aruch. The sec-
Mutnansky deals with an entirely different subject and does not contain the phrase

arbitrarily compiled from the thousands of pages of the Shulchan Aruch one hun-
he called *Der "Judenspiegel"* (the Jewish law code). Needless to say, Justus' addi-
ds "of Christians" occurs nowhere in the original, which refers specifically to idol

Seyss-Inquart. It is known that Andrej Hlinka's policies had been openly anti-
he advent of the anti-clerical Nazi regime in that country.

ast of January 1, 1939, and others.

f December 4, 1938.

Seyss-Inquart.

r, *Zur politischen Entwicklung*, frame 442383.

of this information wished to remain anonymous.

ehler, Tu Rissky Vysielac Vieden," *Rundpost,* June 17, 1939.

nformation sheet dating from early 1938, in Handakten Seyss-Inquart.

ie Slowakei, p. 60.

ek, *Zrada a Pad* (Prague: statni nakladtelstvi Politicke Literatury, 1958), p. 107.
ar Petreas, *Die Slowakei im Umbruch* (Turcianske St. Martin: Kompas, 1941), p.

Tuka's involvement and the role of Mutnansky in the following account is taken
. Oddo, *Slovakia and its People* (New York; Speller, 1960), p. 282.

o, *Maly Slovnik Slovenskeho Statu*, (Bratislava 1965), p. 132.

utnansky, *Tu rissky vysielac Vieden*, (Vienna: Julius Lichtner, 1939), p. 5.

given to the author, July 1969.

I, footnote 13.

Seyss-Inquart.

December 1944 he was appointed the Hlinka Guards' expert for evacuation
questions and served until April 1945 as chairman of the evacuation section in
the Guards' headquarters. At war's end he fled from the advancing Russians
and was interned by the American army along with many other former Nazi
officials in Glasenbach, Austria, on August 17, 1945. From there he was ex-
tradited to Czechoslovakia. Tried before a Czechoslovak court on May 8, 1948,
he was sentenced to twenty years in prison for his wartime activity and was
released on probation on May 16, 1963, after serving fifteen years of his
sentence.[33]

One of the most important questions regarding Mutnansky's activity concerns
the amount of independence he enjoyed in writing his broadcasts.

Mutnansky himself declared in the first of his two books on the subject of
the broadcasts that he was given a free rein by the Germans.[34] His former
superior, Dr. Muehlberger, confirms that Mutnansky wrote his broadcasts independently.[35]

On the other hand there is considerable information available showing that
the actual freedom enjoyed by Mutnansky, or by any other writer, was
overestimated. It is more accurate to say that Mutnansky could write his own
broadcasts within a fairly well-defined propaganda framework established by
his superiors. The existence of such a framework can be seen from
Muehlberger's report on the broadcasts referred to when discussing broadcasting purposes.[36] Also there was available a general program for the broadcasts following November 18 and 19, 1938, apparently drawn up by
Muehlberger for the first few broadcasts after control of his operation had
been transferred to Seyss-Inquart.[37] This document, which states that beginning
November 20 ideological propaganda on National Socialist racial doctrine was
to be started coupled with a careful anti- clerical campaign, shows clearly that
it is correct to assume the existence of a general framework. Obeying these
directives, however, certainly cannot have caused Mutnansky any problems
keeping in mind his enthusiastic pro-Nazi and pro-German attitudes.[38]

There is also no doubt whatsoever about the complete control exercised by
the German government as to who could speak on the Slovak programs. One
contemporary author mentions Dr. Hammerschmid, Seyss-Inquart's aide, as
putting Radio Vienna at the disposal of Karol Murgas during that man's visit
to Vienna in March 1939.[39] There is even evidence of prior censorship of
Murgas's subsequent broadcast.[40]

Mention has already been made that Mutnansky's appointment as announcer of the Slovak broadcasts had the approval of the propaganda
ministry,[41] and there is at least one document of the period in which Dr. Flor,
Seyss-Inquart's second Slovak expert, is quoted as referring to Mutnansky as
"our radio announcer," all of which is evidence of German control.

It can thus be summarized that the actual writing of each broadcast was within Mutnansky's own province but that he almost certainly received periodic instructions on the general content of the broadcasts. It is further certain that the operation of the Slovak program was under complete control of the German authorities and that Slovaks speaking on it could do so only with the expressed approval of the German government.

It might be added that Hammerschmid's putting Radio Vienna at the disposal of Murgas is in poignant contrast to Seyss-Inquart's protestation to Karol Sidor that he had no control over Radio Vienna.[43] If any doubt were left on the subject of Seyss-Inquart's control being very real, this should be dispelled by his letter to Ribbentrop asking about instructions on whether he should include a Czech language program on the Vienna Radio.[44] Obviously the man who had the authority to order the insertion of such programs was also very much in control over them. Seyss-Inquart's answer to Sidor must be seen then as nothing but diplomatic pretense.

Dr. Wolfgang Muehlberger.

The person of Mutnansky's superior in the broadcasting hierarchy of the Vienna Radio station is of particular interest because from every indication it was he who translated German propaganda policy toward Slovakia into the general framework within which Mutnansky would then write his broadcasts. Muehlberger was apparently selected for this position because he was well versed both in the field of propaganda and in Slavic languages. Intellectually he was by far Mutnansky's superior, and there is little doubt that he was the brains of all the Eastern European broadcasting propaganda emanating from Vienna in 1938 and 1939. This becomes evident upon reading his report on the broadcasts of October 1938 defining their purpose[45] and his appraisal of the effects of the broadcasts written in February 1939.[46]

Dr. Wolfgang Muehlberger was born in 1907 in Friedland (current Czech spelling is Frydlant), in the German-speaking part of northwestern Czechoslovakia. He received most of his higher education during the Czechoslovak era, studied at Prague University, and from a fairly early age seems to have belonged to the strongly nationalistic wing of Sudeten Germans. He taught journalism at Leipzig University until he was asked to take over the direction of the Southeast European broadcasts in Vienna in August 1938. While in Vienna his formal title was that of deputy director of South European broadcasts of Radio Vienna, his immediate superior being the intendant, or director, of Radio Vienna, Karl Mages.[47]

His political views already characterized as strongly German-nationalistic, were also anti-Czech and anti-clerical. In line with these basic characteristics he naturally sided with the pro-German wing among the Vienna Slovaks. When in 1940 he became press attache of the German legation in Bratislava, these

leanings continued, and it seems that he
Vojtech Tuka during his service in Slova

When Slovakia was invaded by the Rus
fled to Austria where he was interned by
He was released in 1947 and presently

[1]Handakten
[2]See broadc
[3]Documents
Archives, Wa
[4]Broadcasts
[5]See Tuka's
[6]Another in
which quotes
[7]Karol Sido
22.
[8]Kovar, "N
[9]Documents
Stationery Off
[10]See referen
[11]Documents
[12]See Murga
[13]A clerical,
People's Party
[14]Document
[15]Informatic
[16]Wolfgang
2003, roll 114
[17]Z.A.B. Ze
[18]This refers
tion quoted by
he uses.
[19]Dr. Justus
dred laws whic
tion of the wo
worship.
[20]Handakten
German after
[21]See broad
[22]Broadcast
[24]Handakten
[25]Muehlberg
[26]The sourc
[27]Wilhelm S
[28]Unsigned
[29]Hoensch,
[30]Imrich Sta
[31]Johann Os
69.
[32]The fact o
from Gilbert
[33]Jozef Chr
[34]Ludovit M
[35]Informati
[36]See Chapt
[37]Handakte

[38]For evidence of his prompt compliance with the instructions referred to see the broadcast of November 22, 1938.

[39]Petreas, *Die Slowakei im Umbruch*, p. 171.

[40]See Chapter VIII, footnote 18.

[41]Hoensch, *Die Slowakei*, p. 60.

[42]Memorandum of telephone conversation of January 9, 1939, in Handakten Seyss-Inquart.

[53]See Chapter VIII, footnote 17.

[44]Letter of June 22, 1938, in Handakten Seyss-Inquart.

[45]Muehlberger, *Arbeits-und Organisationsvericht*, in Handakten Seyss-Inquart.

[46]Muehlberger, *Zür politischen Entwicklung*.

[47]Mages had been in charge of the radio station in the Saar area and was brought to Vienna by Buerckel when he was made Gauleiter of the Ostmark following the German annexation of Austria in March 1938.

CHAPTER III

INTERNAL OPPOSITION TO THE BROADCASTS

INTERVENTION AGAINST THE BROADCASTS

During the six-month period between the Munich Agreement and the complete absorption of Czechoslovakia into the German orbit there were several interventions or protests intended either to change the content of the broadcasts or to do away with them altogether. The large number of such interventions is quite impressive and indicates that the broadcasts were indeed a factor to be reckoned with as they would otherwise not have evoked the amount of opposition that is evidenced by the protests.

Curiously enough the very first intervention came from Secretary of State Ernst von Weizsaecker of the German Foreign Office whose task, following the Munich Agreement, was to preside over the international commission appointed by the Munich signatories to implement the provisions of the treaty. Realizing that German propaganda broadcasts in Czech language were likely to stir anew the troubles that had just been "adjusted" by the Munich Agreement, Weizsaecker asked on October 4, 1938, that these broadcasts be subjected to Foreign Office censorship.[1] It is not clear whether he did so honestly to maintain peace and tranquility in Czechoslovakia or merely as a maneuver designed to disassociate the German government from the broadcasts. This latter explanation would fit well with Weizsaecker's attempts as late as March 14, 1939, to convince the British ambassador in Berlin, Sir Nevile Henderson, that "Austria was largely independent of Berlin and often took a line contrary to official German policy."[2] Whatever the explanation for Weizsaecker's move, his suggestion never seems to have been implemented, and German propaganda direction continued to serve ends that were often diametrically opposed to the peace-keeping type of censorship which must have been in the minds of members of the International Commission.

Another protest against the broadcasts, again from a surprising source, is mentioned in the German documents of the period. It seems that in early January 1939, the Slovak government was earnestly seeking to pacify the heated German reaction to a census Tiso had ordered taken at the end of 1938. The government turned to Dr. Tuka, whose friendship with Mutnansky and the Vienna propagandists was probably known, and asked that he intervene against the tone which the broadcasts had at that time assumed. Tuka did so and, quoting the German memorandum, he "asked our announcer Mutnansky not to use such harsh language on the radio since everything is being done on the Slovak side to restore the old good relations."³ It appears that Tuka's intervention was successful and that the sharp anti-Tiso sentiments voiced by Radio Vienna following the census soon gave way to the relations that had existed before.

An interesting protest against a particular item in the broadcasts originated from Alexander Mach, the propaganda chief in the Tiso government. It came a few days after Tuka's intervention and dealt with a radio news item in which a meeting was reported between Mach and George F. Kennan, then secretary of the American legation in Prague. The meeting apparently dealt with the need to allow more Slovaks to emigrate to the United States. Mach was embarrassed by this report because it conflicted with the outwardly optimistic stance of the Slovak government which even spoke of making it possible for Slovak emigrants to return home once their country was properly managed by an autonomous (or independent) government.⁴ The Vienna radio published Mach's protest but maintained a self-righteous attitude by pointing out that *Slovak,* the newspaper of Mach's own party, had also reported on the meeting with Kennan. From the Slovak broadcast of January 13, 1939 (Chapter VII) it will be seen what clever use was made of the whole issue by Mutnansky to turn the ire of his Slovak listeners against the Jews and - without saying so outright - against the Czechs. Also, he used the incident to create bad feelings against moderates in the Slovak government who, he implied, sacrificed the well-being of their fellow countrymen to protect Czechs and Jews.

On March 4, 1939, Prime Minister Tiso addressed a telegram to Seyss-Inquart asking that the Slovak language program on Radio Vienna be discontinued. Tiso's step was on the highest level of all the various interventions and protests. It read as follows:

> On the basis of the authority granted to me on February 14, 1939, by the government of Slovakia. I take the liberty of requesting you to order the liquidation of Slovak broadcasts on Radio Vienna since the form of the broadcasts is such as to disturb the consolidation of Slovak conditions. Will you accept, Mr. Reichsstatthalter, the expression of my profound esteem.
> Dr. Jozef Tiso
> Chairman of the Slovak Government⁵

In spite of (or perhaps because of) the importance of this protest, nothing but the bare facts of the telegram can be found in the German files. The telegram must be viewed against the background of Czech- Slovak discussions which had begun in Prague on March 1 and 2. In these discussions the future of the two nations' relations was being discussed with considerable frankness on both sides, and it was obviously in the Germans' interest to prevent a favorable outcome of these discussions. This would go far to explain reports carried by

Radio Vienna on the very day of the telegram to the effect that the Prague government was sending troop reinforcements to Slovakia.[6] On March 2 another broadcast had stressed the independence movement in Slovakia.[7] Another report on Czech troop movements followed on March 7, a few days after the events described here, and was promptly denied by the newspaper *Slovak,* thus giving further evidence that this was indeed a highly sensitive issue in Slovakia. It is obvious that the German propagandists relished any news that would enable them to fan Czech-Slovak enmity. It is equally obvious that the Slovak government had nothing to gain from such enmity and was bound to resent anything that tended to exaggerate the importance of the animosity between Prague and Bratislava which undoubtedly did exist at the moment.

The protest of Karol Sidor against Murgas's attack on him on Radio Vienna will be discussed in connection with that broadcast.[9] It was the last intervention prior to Slovak independence.

Following the occupation of Bohemia and Moravia by the German army in March 1939, the German High Command opposed the continuation of Czech language broadcasts, but the ban was lifted again when Karl Hermann Frank became state secretary for Bohemia and Moravia.[10] It will be remembered that Frank most likely was the man who had picked Muehlberger to direct the broadcasts. At any rate, the German army opposition had no effect on Slovak language broadcasts but seems to have applied only to broadcasts in Czech which were beamed at western Czechoslovakia.

In completing this brief review of the various protests launched against the broadcasts, mention should be made here of Ferdinand Durcansky's opposition to the scheme of putting Mutnansky in charge of a new Slovak broadcast series from Kattowitz at the end of 1939.

It is significant that the German authorities had a long memory for those who had at any time opposed the broadcasts. Their files contain a list of Slovak public figures, including Palo Carnogursky, who had replied over Radio Bratislava to Karol Murgas's broadcast against his friend Sidor in the critical days of March 1939. This list describes Carnogursky as a man who had "compromised himself at the time of the Czech coup in favor of Prague and who had taken a particularly strong stand against the Vienna Slovak broadcasts."[12] In other words, opposition to the Vienna Slovak broadcasts was by that time considered as tantamount to being pro-Prague and anti-German.

OPPOSITION TO MUTNANSKY

Reference has been made to the fact that Mutnansky's radio attacks earned him the personal enmity of a number of leading figures in Slovak politics, and there is ample evidence of steps taken by some of these to remove Mutnansky from his position on Radio Vienna. There are even indications that Mutnansky and his friend Vavra, the Slovak consul in Vienna, were under surveillance by the Tiso government.

The German files contain one revealing report regarding Prime Minister Tiso's protest to Karol Sidor about frequent meetings of Sidor's secretary with Mutnansky. The report is undated, but it seems fairly certain that it originated in the period of Sidor's ascendancy in the last two months of 1938 or the first two months of 1939. Sidor refused to interfere and declared that the meetings were strictly of a romantic nature and not due to any attempt by Mutnansky to gain access to government secrets, which Tiso obviously feared was the case.[13] The incident shows not only that Mutnansky was being watched by the Slovak government, but also that he must at that time have circulated rather freely between Bratislava and Vienna, unless it is assumed that Sidor's secretary met him on German soil. The fact that the protest was known to the Germans shows the effectiveness of their espionage.

While this incident had no consequences, a far more serious attack against Mutnansky followed less than half a year after Slovak independence had been achieved. From the curt description of the SD files it would appear that the Slovak government asked the German government in early August 1939 to remove Mutnansky from his position and that the Germans agreed. The pretext for the Slovak demand was Mutnansky's criminal record which apparently was not unknown to the SD officials reporting the case. For the following year or more several attempts were made by the Vienna Slovaks, supported evidently by the SD, to reinstate Mutnansky, but none of these efforts succeeded. In December 1939 a plan to use Mutnansky for a series of Slovak broadcasts on the German radio station Kattowitz was rejected by Durcansky who was then foreign minister of Slovakia. Mutnansky's activity at this point consisted of directing the Hlinka Guard's Foreign Legion of which, it will be remembered, he was in command. Here, too, efforts were made to oppose Mutnansky by dissolving the entire Foreign Legion. Slovak Propaganda Chief Mach was reportedly planning to do this in February 1940, and a later report from October 1940 mentions that he had not lost sight of this plan,[14] and apparently carried it out shortly thereafter. Mach's attitude may have been due to opposition to Mutnansky, but it is more likely that the Slovak government found that the Hlinka Guard's Foreign Legion lent itself particularly well to being used as an instrument through which Germany could influence, pressure, and infiltrate Slovakian politics, and especially so since it was led by men like Mutnansky or Vavra who worked for Germany rather than for their own country. In other words, it was opposition to Mutnansky, but even more importantly the desire to remain masters in their own house that prompted these Slovak moves. The final outcome was most likely to remove Mutnansky from his last position of power, a position from which he might have endangered what Slovakian independence there was.[15]

[1]Political Files, Bonn Foreign Office, "Durchfuehrung des Muenchener Abkommens," File pol. IV, Microfilm.

[2]*Documents on British Foreign Policy,* vol. IV, no. 235.

[3]Handakten Seyss-Inquart.

[4]Handakten Seyss-Inquart; see also *Voelkiscer Beobachter,* Vienna edition. January 13, 1939, p. 5.

[5]Handakten Seyss-Inquart.

[6]See broadcast of March 4, 1939.

[7]See broadcast of March 2, 1939.

[8]Petreas, *Die Slowakei im Umbruch* p. 153.

[9]See Murgas' broadcast of March 13, 1939.

[10]Handakten Seyss-Inquart.

[11]Documents of the SD-Leitabschnitt Vienna.

[12]Handakten Seyss-Inquart; see also comments on Murgas broadcast of March 13, 1939.

[13]Handakten Seyss-Inquart.

[14]Documents of the SD-Leitabschnitt Vienna. Also: Microfilm T-175, Roll 556, frames 9432441-43.

[15]Professor Y. Jelinek in a letter to the author emphasizes that Mutnansky was fully compensated for being dropped from Radio Vienna by his appointment as social attache at the Slovak legation in Berlin. For further evidence regarding the enmity between Mutnansky and Mach reference should be made to Culen's biograpy of Dr. Tiso where he quotes Tiso's statement during his trial that Mach at one time had Mutnansky arrested. (Konstantin Culen: *Po Svatoplukovi druha nasa hlava,* Middletown, Pennsylvania, Jednota Printery, 1947, p. 414).

CHAPTER IV

INTERNATIONAL REACTION TO THE BROADCASTS

The following description of reactions from abroad to the Vienna broadcasts has been confined to the published official diplomatic records of some of the nations listed. It is not intended to be a complete record of such reactions but rather to give some indication of the interpretations given to the broadcasts by various diplomatic missions in Czechoslovakia or Germany. As will be seen, much of the reaction dates from the days immediately preceding the dismemberment of Czechoslovakia in March 1939.

British. From the point of view of volume, British diplomatic reports paid far greater attention to Czechoslovak events than did those of the French, Italian, or United States missions in Berlin or Prague.

The first warning about the broadcasts was given to the British government by its Prague legation on November 1, 1938. In its dispatch of that day the fact was stressed that the broadcasts were encouraging Slovak separatism.[1] The next warning significantly did not come until March 10, 1939, a few days before the collapse of Czechoslovakia, when the British Embassy in Berlin reported that the Czech military attache in Berlin had warned his British colleague that Radio Vienna was fomenting trouble between Czechs and Slovaks.[2] From then on the Vienna broadcasts were in the forefront of diplomatic attention, and on March 11 the Prague legation sent two dispatches giving details of Ferdinand Durcansky's speech of March 10 and calling attention to the fact that Durcansky was using the Vienna radio for his attacks against the Czechs.[3] The following day the Prague legation reported that Durcansky was to have spoken again on March 11 but that no speech had been audible "perhaps owing to interruptions." The actual reason, as we now know, had been the postponement of Slovak independence due to the stubborn resistance of Karol Sidor to German pressure for a declaration of independence.[4] On March 13, the British Embassy in Berlin reported Vienna's continued transmissions of anti-Czech propaganda in the Slovak language.[5]

French. The first French diplomatic notices of the Vienna broadcasts came from the French Embassy in Berlin and were dated March 14 and March 18, 1939.[6] In the first of these two dispatches Robert Coulondre, the French ambassador, said that German agitation in Slovakia had been ordered about three weeks earlier thus confirming the prevailing misconception that the German campaign in Slovakia, including the radio broadcasts, was of very recent origin.

Polish. An interesting reaction to the broadcasts by Hitler's next victims, the Poles, is contained in an unpublished diplomatic dispatch of the German

charge d'affaires in Prague, Andor Hencke. In a note dated March ll, 1939, he quoted a member of the Polish legation to the effect that Durcansky's speech on Radio Vienna was proof that Germany backed the Slovakian separatists.[7]
Hungarian. The same dispatch of Hencke also mentioned the reaction of the Hungarian minister to Prague who told Hencke that Germany "certainly gave the Slovaks some potent injection treatment" by allowing Durcansky to speak on Radio Vienna.[8]
Italian. The Hencke dispatch also contained the notable reaction of the Italian minister to Prague. Although officially the representative of Germany's closest ally, he was reported by Hencke as saying that he could not understand the purpose of Durcansky's Vienna radio speech and felt that the Slovaks had committed treason against Czechoslovakia.[9]
Czech. Of all the reactions those of the Czechs are naturally the most interesting since it was they who were most directly affected by the events which the broadcasts had helped to stage. The warning of the Czech military attache to his British colleague in Berlin has already been referred to above.[10]

Perhaps the most poignant of many Czech comments of the period appears in another of Hencke's unpublished dispatches. In this dispatch, dated March 13, 1939, he quotes a comment made on Radio Prague at 2200 hours of March 12 to the effect that "history will ostracize the treason of those Slovaks who now spread hate over Radio Vienna."[11]

It may well be asked, however, whether anything was done by the Prague government to jam the Vienna broadcasts. The answer to this question must be subdivided into the period preceding the Munich Agreement when Czechoslovakia was a free country able to defend herself against psychological as well as physical attack, and into the period following Munich when it was politically unwise for Czechoslovakia to provoke Germany. In addition, it appears that any attempt at Czech jamming was bound to remain largely ineffective in view of the superior broadcasting equipment available to the Germans.

Muehlberger's report of October 1938 mentions a Czech prohibition of public listening to the Vienna broadcasts during the days of the Munich crisis as well as the confiscation of radio receivers in western Slovakia. He adds that Czech and Soviet attempts to jam the Vienna broadcasts were only of temporary effect and states that Czech jamming was confined to Prague and a few other major centers in the western part of the country.[12]

Another source of information on the subject of jamming is the London *News Chronicle* which, on April ll, 1939, featured an article by Edgar Weir entitled "Radio Propaganda: the New Weapon of War." The article contained the following: "Quite recently German broadcasting played an important part in the 'liberation of Slovakia.' Without radio the country-wide appeals from Vienna would have been impossible, as the frontiers would have been closed. Slovakia was without the technical means of making Vienna inaudible."[13]

Although the writer seems unaware of any political reluctance which Czech or Slovak governmental authorities may have had against jamming German broadcasts, the information he supplies about the lack of effective jamming capacity in Slovakia confirms Muehlberger's information.

The fact that Durcansky's failure to speak again on March 11 was due to political events and not to jamming has been mentioned above.[14]

It can be concluded then that the Czechs were trying to jam German broadcasts before the Munich Agreement, possibly also later, but that their capacity to do so was no match for the power of the German radio stations surrounding her to the north, west, and south.

TIMELINESS OF REACTION TO BROADCASTS

It will become evident from a brief study of the available material that the reaction of the world at large, and especially that of Czechoslovakia's allies, Britain and France, to the Vienna broadcasts showed the same mixture of unawareness and of unfounded allied optimism that characterizes so much of the Munich period. The attention of the foreign ministries of Britain, France, and the United States, as shown in their diplomatic dispatches, was not directed to the broadcasts emanating from Vienna until the very end of Czechoslovak independence. The broadcasts, as has been shown, had become a daily feature on one of the largest German radio stations as early as September 3, 1938, and had continued from that time on with only one slight interruption in the first half of November. During that time they were used to disrupt the unity of Czechoslovakia, a nation that had been promised a guarantee by the four signatory powers of the Munich Agreement in return for costly concessions made to preserve world peace. The broadcasts were also used to spread racial, political, and ideological hatred amongst the citizens of Czechoslovakia. Yet, as was shown, the first dispatch reporting such unprecedented subvertive propaganda across international borders came only when Sir Basil Newton, the British minister to Prague, on November 1, 1938, called his government's attention to the fact that the Slovaks were being "daily encouraged (to seek independence) by the messages broadcast in Slovak from German stations."[15] No mention of the subject followed until more than a month later when Newton again referred to it, adding his doubts as to whether the Germans really desired an independent Slovakia.[16] Nothing further is heard in British dispatches about the broadcasts until the climactic days of February and March 1939. French, and also American dispatches seem to have paid no attention whatsoever to the broadcasts until March 1939.[17] No wonder statesmen reacted to the German destruction of the rest of Czechoslovakia in March 1939 as if it had come as a complete surprise. In most cases they had not been informed of the broadcasts and of other obvious indications of hostile intentions, or having been so informed they had chosen to give the information received the most optimistic interpretation, thus misleading themselves and their nations.

It would seem that of the entire broadcast series from Vienna to Slovakia between September 1938 and March 1939 only the very final broadcasts received their due share of world attention. For example, of thirteen British dispatches dealing with the subject, all but three date from March 1939,[18] while in the case of the French and American dispatches there was apparently no mention whatever of the broadcasts prior to March 1939.[19] The same is largely true of the press. *The New York Times,* for instance, reported the fact of the Vienna broadcasts for the first time on March 5, 1939. As late as March 10, the well-known correspondent of that paper, G.E.R. Gedye, wrote that a Hungarian attack against Slovakia was reported by Germans in Slovakia, giving no indication at all that he was aware or even suspected that this story was nothing but a German "plant" to cover up their real intentions.

From a purely practical point of view it would have been difficult, if not impossible, for Radio Vienna to attract large numbers of Slovak listeners during those climactic March days had they not built a nucleus of listeners during the preceding six months. The conclusion is justified that even if the broadcasts prior to March 1939 had indeed been unimportant as far as their content was concerned, they more than made up for this in March by the fact that during those six months they had become an accepted and well-known fact in Slovakia. By the time March came many Slovaks who at first refused to listen to the Vienna series probably changed their minds, not from any change of heart but simply because they wanted to get the news from the source that was making the news. Moreover, it would be quite wrong to say that the broadcasts prior to March 1939 were unimportant, as will be seen from their texts and from the discussion of their effects.

OVEROPTIMISTIC INTERPRETATIONS

The Munich era has been characterized as one of wishful dreams on the part of Western European governments. It must now be shown how this attitude led to several wrong interpretations of facts connected with the Vienna broadcasts in the countries endangered by German expansion.

The most fundamental of these misinterpretations was the belief that "Vienna is not Berlin." In other words, the Vienna broadcasts were the work of a small group of Austrian Nazis who acted without the authority of Berlin or who even counteracted Berlin policy.

The only explanation of how mature statesmen, diplomats, or journalists could seriously believe that a rigorous dictatorship like Hitler's would consider allowing any one group of its faithful to make foreign policy on its own is to be found in the fact that Berlin did its best to support such erroneous interpretations to better camouflage its true intentions. As noted earlier, Sir Nevile

Henderson was told by Ernst von Weizsaecker, secretary of state in the German Foreign Ministry, that "Austria was largely independent of Berlin and often took a line contrary to official policy" in Germany.[20] The fact that Weizsaecker told this tale is not nearly as surprising as Henderson's apparent willingness to believe it. Nor is this an isolated incident. The London press held similar beliefs. The *Daily Telegraph and Morning Post* reported in the critical days of March 1939 that Seyss-Inquart may have planned to make Slovakia independent without the knowledge of Berlin.[21]

A brief examination of Seyss-Inquart's actual position may be advisable at this point. There is some indication that he had indeed hoped to be appointed to a leading position in Slovakia after the German takeover of that country. This can be gathered from a letter Dr. Fritz Flor, his assistant and friend, wrote to him on December 20, 1938, reporting on conditions in Slovakia. After discussing the fact that the various German officials involved in Slovak affairs seemed to suffer from extremely poor coordination and recommending that the German minority's paramilitary organization, the FS, be closely coordinated with the German SS, Flor adds the following significant paragraph: "And one more thing: is it not high time that you clarify your future authority or prepare your official position? And also: what happens here in Slovakia whether this be for good or for evil, will be, let us make no mistake about it, credited to your account. That is another reason why I am for clarification of your position."[22]

This revealing passage is fairly clear evidence that Seyss-Inquart did have high ambitions regarding his role in the future of Slovakia at least at the end of 1938. He may not have realized at the time that when the Slovak upheaval, which he had done so much to organize, finally came, it led to complete independence leaving no opening for a high-ranking German official. After Slovakia became independent Seyss-Inquart was briefly considered as ambassador to that country, but this idea was rejected because it would have been a demotion for a man of Seyss's rank in the German hierarchy.[23]

The evidence regarding Seyss-Inquart's actual authority in Slovak affairs prior to Slovak independence is quite conclusive and shows that regardless of any ambitions he may have held, he was strictly under orders to Berlin, foremost of course, under Hitler's orders but also under those of Foreign Minister Ribbentrop. Hitler's orders to Seyss-Inquart to obtain information on Slovak conditions were related by him at the Nuremberg trials.[24] His contacts with Ribbentrop are equally well-documented and show that he was definitely asking for, and accepting, Ribbentrop's orders. Mention has already been made of his letter to Ribbentrop asking about his intentions on Czech language broadcasts from Vienna.[25] Another instance of contact between Ribbentrop and Seyss-Inquart, again clearly indicative of who was giving the orders, dates from November 1938 at which time Vojtech Tuka had been freed from Czech confinement to the Plzen area and had returned to Slovakia. Ribbentrop at that time gave the following order: "Seyss-Inquart is to keep contact with Tuka without taking a stand or 'activating' Tuka."[26]

There are several other indications that Seyss-Inquart's position was clearly subordinate to Berlin. One of these is a letter addressed by him to Ribbentrop on January 17, 1939, asking him to send a Foreign Ministry official to Vienna to coordinate Southeast European contacts.[27] It is also known that Seyss-Inquart's project of founding a Southeastern Institute in Vienna, from which propaganda and other German activities in the Balkans could be directedwas shelved at the insistence of Ribbentrop in the fall of 1938[28] and that Seyss-Inquart docilely admitted later that Ribbentrop's decision had been right.[29]

In short, it can be reiterated that while Seyss-Inquart did at one time have some fairly high ambitions in regard to Slovakia, his position and actions were those of a man in charge of Slovak affairs for the German government. There is not the slightest evidence that he ever made policy on his own. In fact, there is every indication that any attempt to do so under the Hitler regime was tantamount to signing one's death warrant and this latter fact should, by 1939, have been known to everyone supposedly familiar with German affairs. If men like Henderson could nevertheless allow themselves to be misled, the only explanation that can be found lies in the false optimism and wishful thinking of the Munich era.

A similar misinterpretation which should also be mentioned was that the German campaign for Slovak independence was nothing more than an attempt to make the Czechs more compliant to German wishes. This was the gist of a report of *The New York Times* on the Slovak situation dated March 9, 1939. While this interpretation might have been accurate at the time preceding the Munich Agreement, it seems clear that the author of the article was not aware that Germany by March 1939 possessed much more direct methods of pressuring the Czechs, and that it was scarcely logical to assume that she would have schemed and worked for Slovak independence for half a year or more merely to coax the Czechs into being more accessible to their wishes.

[1]*Documents on British Foreign Policy,* vol. III, no. 245.

[2]Ibid., vol. IV, no. 197.

[3]Ibid., vol. III, nos. 208 and 212. See also Durcansky broadcast of March 10, 1939.

[4]Ibid., vol. IV, no. 215.

[5]*Documents on British Foreign Policy,* vol. IV, no. 225. For a complete list of all British dispatches dealing with the Vienna broadcasts, see footnote 18 of this chapter.

[6]*French Yellow Book,* nos. 65 and 79.

[7]Milan Stanislao Durica, *La Slovacchia e le sue Relazioni Politiche con la Germania 1938-1945* (Padova: Marsilio Editori, 1964), p. 172, quoting Hencke's dispatch no. 64.

[8]Ibid.

[9]Ibid.

[10]*Documents on British Foreign Policy,* vol. IV, no. 197.

[11]Durica, *La Slovacchia e le sue Relazioni Politiche,* p. 172, quoting Hencke's dispatch no. 105 of March 13, 1939.

[12]Muehlberger, *Arbeits- und Organisationsbericht,* in Handakten Seyss-Inquart.

[13]*News Chronicle,* London, April 11, 1939.

[14]*Documents on British Foreign Policy,* vol. IV, no. 215.

[15]*Documents on British Foreign Policy,* vol. III, no. 245.

[16]*Ibid.,* vol. III, no. 413.

[17]*French Yellow Book,* nos. 65 and 79, of March 14 and 18, 1939, respective-For American dispatches see George F. Kennan, *From Prague after Munich* (Princeton: Princeton University Press, 1968), p. 78 (dispatch of March 9, 1939).

[18]The dispatches are the following, taken from *Documents on British Foreign Policy.* Vol. III: no. 245, Nov. 1, 1938; no. 413, Dec. 8, 1938. Vol. IV: no. 97, Feb. 9, 1939; no. 188, Mar. 8, 1939; nos. 197 and 200, Mar. 10, 1939; nos. 208 an 212, Mar. 11, 1939; no. 215, Mar. 12, 1939; nos. 225 and 230, Mar. 13, 1939; no. 235, Mar. 14, 1939; no. 450, Mar. 20, 1939.

[19]*French Yellow Book,* nos. 65 and 79, of March 14 and 18, 1939, respectively. In the second of the French dispatches reference is made to the agitation in Slovakia having been ordered three weeks ago thus increasing the likelihood that the writer of the dispatch was unaware that it had begun several months prior to that date.

[20]*Documents on British Foreign Policy,* vol. IV, no. 235.

[21]Handakten Seyss-Inquart, referring to issue of March 13, p. 13.

[22]Handakten Seyss-Inquart, referring to issue of March 13, p. 13.

[23]Davidson, *The Trial of the Germans* (New York: MacMillan, 1966), p. 456.

[24]*Trial of the Major War Criminals,* Nuremberg, 1947, vol. XV, p. 637.

[25]See Chapter I, footnote 10.

[26]Political Archives, Bonn Foreign Office, Microfilm T-120; see also

Hoensch, *Die Slowakei,* p. 213, footnote 19.

[27]Handakten Seyss-Inquart.

[28]Ibid; letter by Seyss-Inquart to Heydrich dated November 18, 1938.

[29]Ibid., letter by Seyss-Inquart dated January 17, 1939.

CHAPTER V

THE EFFECT OF THE BROADCASTS

The crucial question for the student of the Vienna broadcasts is, of course, how much of an effect they had on Czechoslovak events in March 1939. An important contribution to answering this question is made by Muehlberger in his report of February 1939 describing conditions in Slovakia. The report dwells at length on the various factions within the Slovak political leadership and deplores the fact that due to lack of experience, character, or initiative the majority of public figures in charge of Slovak affairs were simply not qualified for their jobs. Muehlberger's report must be viewed as a highly subjective one in the sense that he was interested in those factions of Slovak leadership backing Germany. These were primarily the group around Tuka, consisting of Tuka himself, Propaganda Chief Mach, and possibly Matus Cernak,[1] and a second group consolidated around Sidor. (It must be noted that in February 1939 Sidor had not as yet done anything to oppose German aims and was still considered by the Germans as Slovakia's coming man.) The Sidor group was comprised of Murgas and the brothers Anton and Karol Mederly. Durcansky was seen by Muehlberger as pro-German but politically in a class all by himself.

This completes what Muehlberger considered to be the pro-German political leadership of Slovakia. There was another far more numerous group which had formed around Tiso and was supported by the clergy, the Christian labor unions led by the anti-German Cavojsky, and, in addition, the bulk of the Slovak farmers who were firmly oriented around the church.

A last group consisted of what Muehlberger calls the Czechoslovaks, that is, the men who had remained outspokenly loyal to Prague and to the idea of a central state. One member of the Slovak government was seen by Muehlberger as belonging to this group, namely Minister of Economics Pavel Teplansky.[2]

To reiterate briefly, Muehlberger's report is full of pessimism because its author saw the situation very clearly and recognized that the majority of the nation backed Tiso rather than the pro- German element around Tuka. Had Muehlberger known when he wrote his report that Sidor would oppose the German demands for a declaration of independence when the chips were down, he would undoubtedly have been even more pessimistic.

What this estimation of the situation indicates regarding the broadcasts is stated very well by the official of the National Socialist Party's foreign affairs section to whom Muehlberger had addressed his report. In forwarding Muehlberger's report to the Foreign Ministry he wrote as follows:

> . . .From the enclosed report of Dr. Muehlberger it will be seen that certain decisions are to be expected in Slovakia during the month of March. Most importantly the relations to Prague are to be clarified. One is almost inclined to doubt whether the Slovaks by themselves

have sufficient strength for that struggle. In addition the Slovak government is far from united and men like Sidor and Durcansky, who it would appear would be forced into a common front against Tiso, are like cat and dog. Undoubtedly Dr. Tuka must be seen as a very positive factor at the present time.[3]

This revealing document interprets Muehlberger's pessimistic findings quite correctly as indicating that the pro-German, pro-separatist element in Slovakia was not strong enough numerically, nor sufficiently united, nor perhaps, of sufficient conviction to strike a blow for independence as Germany wished them to do.

What conclusions does this allow regarding the effectiveness of the Vienna broadcasts? Should they now be interpreted as having been utterly useless? Before answering this question, additional sources need to be searched to ascertain whether they corroborate Muehlberger's report, keeping in mind that Muehlberger had excellent information at his disposal from his constant study of the Slovak news media, from inside information coming out of Slovakia to which he undoubtedly had access, from comments of Slovak listeners, etc. Even more importantly, he stood to gain from drawing an optimistic picture and to lose by drawing a pessimistic one, so that if any bias were to be expected from him, it was much more likely to be in the direction of overoptimism rather than the opposite.

One fact that corroborates Muehlberger's views, though perhaps it does so in an indirect fashion, is Sidor's resistance to German demands during his premiership in March 1939. It is highly unlikely that he would have held out against German pressure as long as he did had he felt the bulk of his countrymen to be actively opposed to his action and not backing him.

In line with this argument there is the fact that there was not a trace of a Slovak popular uprising against Prague in March 1939, which the Germans were working quite hard to provoke.[4] One author, who has studied the period in great detail, has this comment on the reaction to Durcansky's and to Murgas's appeals on Radio Vienna for a Slovak rising: "The effect of their summons evaporated. The popular reaction was apathetic."[5] A document in Seyss-Inquart's personal file dating from February 1939, the authorship of which is unknown, stated that the Vienna program in Slovakia "is being treated by Slovaks as the organ of the extreme wing of the Hlinka Guards and is sharply rejected by moderates."[6] All the facts marshalled so far point in the direction of Slovak apathy regarding the German-supported independence movement. It may be worthwhile, in view of such unanimity of evidence, to listen to what the backers of the Vienna broadcasts have said on this subject. One of these supporters is Dr. Tuka whose views were written in the form of a foreword to Mutnansky's books where he likened the broadcasts' effect to that of "Big Bertha."[7] Mutnansky tells his readers that he had a discussion with Tuka early in November 1938 during which Tuka coined the phrase the "revolution on radio waves" for Mutnansky's activity in Vienna.[8] This phrase was later used as the title for Mutnansky's second book. It is highly questionable, though, whether this phrase was much more than wishful thinking on Tuka's part. Besides, he could not possibly have foreseen the results of Mutnansky's activity at the time he coined the phrase. It is one thing for Mutnansky to feel flattered by this epithet, but it is quite another to ascribe historic truth to it since Slovak independence was anything but a true revolution. If the term revolution must be applied at all cost, it might be called a revolution from the top, strongly influenced by German pressure. Tuka's phrase thus cannot be taken for much more than an optimistic and flattering slogan.

Another laudatory article on Mutnansky's work, written in a German radio magazine in June 1939,[9] has much to say about Mutnansky's separatist propaganda when Slovakia was still committed to a policy of autonomy; but the article does not make any claims for the effect of the broadcasts on the course of Slovak events. The same is largely true of an article published in the organ of the Hlinka Guards' *Gardista* in February 1942, which praises Mutnansky's pro- independence stand as well as his anti-Semitic and anti-Masonic views but makes no claims regarding the political effectiveness of the broadcast series.[10]

In the light of these facts and claims the following conclusions appear justified. It is quite clear that the Vienna Slovak broadcasts and other German propaganda ventures did not succeed in setting in motion a genuine Slovak independence movement, or a movement aimed at overthrowing the remnants of Czech control over Slovak affairs. This does not necessarily indicate, however, that the broadcasts did not contribute to the neutralization of Slovak sentiments of loyalty to the Czechoslovak state. The neutralization process, which resulted in Slovak apathy when the Czechoslovak state was destroyed by Germany in March 1939, was brought about by, among other things, the following methods:

> - Promises of a better future economically and a safer future politically if Slovaks sided with Germany and divorced themselves from the "adventurers" in Prague.
> - Constant agitation designed to disunite what had formerly been a fairly homogeneous patriotic group. This agitation appealed to sentiments of hate (anti-Semitic, anti-Masonic, anti-Czech), fear (of military attack by Germany), and self-pity.
> - Use of public ostracism and prolonged, concentrated invective directed against all who opposed the policies favored by the propagandists.

In addition to being a vehicle for the propaganda methods just enumerated the broadcasts served as a source of straightforward information that might not otherwise have been available to the Slovak public. Even though this information may have been truthful and devoid of propaganda, its selection and the timing of its presentation were bound to be such as to support the effects of the broadcasts' propaganda aims.

From what has been shown a few general conclusions can now be made.

The cumulative effect of the glowing picture drawn of independence coupled with threats, cajolery, and hate-mongering, used by the Vienna broadcasts and by other German propaganda media, was considerable in disuniting the Slovak people. While this effect was not powerful enough to propel the Slovaks to change sides and to start an armed insurrection against the Prague government as Germany obviously intended, it was nevertheless of considerable influence on Slovak developments in the sense that it reduced Slovak pro-Czechoslovak sentiment to the point of complete apathy. By eroding support for the Czechoslovak state as it had formerly existed, German propaganda was definitely a factor in rendering the vast masses of Slovakia unwilling and unable to resist the destruction of that state in its hour of deadly peril.

In other words, it is true to say that the broadcasts and other German propaganda efforts were not a complete success since they never attained their maximum goal of an armed Slovak uprising against Prague; but they must be credited for a very large partial success in the sense that the Slovak apathy they induced enabled Germany to impose her own solutions without resistance and with the passive compliance of the Slovak people.

[1]Matus Cernak was the leader of the Hlinka Youth Movement.

[2]Muehlberger, *Zur politischen Entwicklung.*

[3]Document signed by Buettner and preceding Muehlberger's report referred to in footnote 2, frame 442380.

[4]Of the many documents on this subject one of the best is in *British Documents on Foreign Policy.* Third Series, vol. IX, No. 450. It contains the account of the March crisis by the British consul in Bratislava.

[5]Helmuth K. G. Roennefarth, *Die Sudetenkrise in der Internationalen Politik* (Wiesbaden: Franz Steiner Verlag GMBH, 1961), p. 733.

[6]Handakten Seyss-Inquart.

[7]See Tuka's foreword to Mutnansky's books.

[8]Ludovit Mutnansky, *Slovenska Revolucia na Vlnach Eteru* (Bratislava: Nakladom vlastnym, 1942), p. 32.

[9]Stiehler, "Tu Rissky Vysielac Vieden."

[10]*Gardista,* February 13, 1942.

CHAPTER VI

THE PRE-MUNICH BROADCASTS

The Vienna broadcasts to Czechoslovakia started on September 3, 1938, almost a full month before the Munich Agreement was signed.[1] For a few days these broadcasts, for which the Germans had rather cleverly chosen the Czechoslovak national motto *Pravda Vitazi* (The Truth Will Win), seem to have been made only in the Czech language, and no attempt was made to single out the Slovaks in a separate program with a distinct appeal. This changed by September 15, however, at which time a special Slovak language program, announced by Ludovit Mutnansky, was started. Mutnansky headed this program until August 1939.

Fortunately a relatively large number of these earliest Slovak language broadcasts were later published by Mutnansky, and they give us a good idea of the political content of these pre-Munich programs. Not surprisingly the emphasis from the very beginning was on Slovak separatism. In the warlike atmosphere of the days preceding the Munich Agreement it was quite natural for the Germans to use every weapon at their disposal to destroy Czechoslovak unity. What should have caused far more of a surprise among Czechoslovakia's allies, however, was that these separatist appeals not only were allowed to continue after the Munich Agreement, but that they became more strident in tone as time went on.

Slovak broadcast of September 17, 1938.

This is Radio Vienna's program of Slovak news: Truth Will Win.

Dear fellow countrymen! In response to many requests we are broadcasting to you in the Slovak language. Why? Because it is necessary to counter the false information which the so-called Slovak radio is feeding you every day. In view of the seriousness of the times and of our situation it is imperative that Slovaks be given a clear picture of developments. To give an example, CTK (the Czechoslovak news agency) reported this morning that there were no serious incidents, that the situation is quiet, and that the news reports of German radio stations, especially of Radio Vienna, are mere inventions.

Let us compare this statement with the report that martial law had to be extended to as many as sixteen Czechoslovak districts. This throws a curious light on the men in Prague who are wielding power. How does extension of martial law rhyme with the calm that is supposed to prevail? The report that all is quiet is further discredited in today's Czech and Slovak newspapers such as *Venkov* and *Slovak*. They report several bloody incidents in the border areas. The dissatisfaction with the stand taken by the Prague government is spreading and has now led to dissatisfaction among large groups of the population of Central Bohemia. Slovakia, too, is in a similar condition to that of the border areas of Bohemia, Moravia, and Silesia as can be seen from the sudden rise of food prices, the lack of confidence in the currency, and from the cessation of payments by several banks. The consequence of this is that the terrorism used by the central authorities is increasing, that Jewish money flows to strengthen the bastions of Marxism, and that the government tries to create faits accompli by sudden actions. Thus many Slovak reservists who had been called to the colors in the last few days were taken to Bohemia and put under the supervision of Czech officers in the Sudeten[2] area as if they were traitors. Slovakia was thus robbed of her sons in order to facilitate the work of the Red Terror.

Even now Red arsonists are preparing to create incidents in Slovakia similar to those in the historic areas.[3] Slovak soldiers refused to fire on defenseless inhabitants of the Sudeten areas, and a large number of them escaped into Germany in full uniform. It is more important than ever today to find out the true facts of the current situation.

Source: Mutnansky, *Slovenska Revolucia na Vlnach Eteru,* pp. 16.17. This book will henceforth be referred to as *Slovenska Revolucia.*

This earliest of broadcasts whose content is known clearly showed several of the features of the many that were to follow. These were: 1. The tendency to equate the Czech government with Marxism. 2. A strong anti-Semitic tone that was to become vicious as time went on. 3. An attempt to make the cause of the German minority in Czechoslovakia and of the Slovaks who, at least theoretically, held the status of equal partners, rather than that of a minority group, to appear identical in the sense that both national groups, the Germans and the Slovaks, were depicted as victims of Czech tyranny. There is no doubt that this was an effective propaganda device from the German point of view as long as Germany, before Munich, tried to win as many allies as possible against the Czechs. After Munich it was to be an equally effective device for the Slovak separatist leadership in its appeal to the then victorious Germans for help against the Prague government.

In addition to the appearance of these standard features, there is one more aspect of the broadcast that calls for comment. This is the seemingly paradoxical situation of the announcer condemning the Czechs for treating Slovak soldiers as traitors, while reporting at the very next moment that Slovaks were deserting to Germany. While this may not be good logic, it is still effective propaganda since in times of tension such as those preceding Munich. Slovaks inclined to extreme nationalism - to whom these broadcasts were primarily directed - were likely to accept such arguments without applying standards of logic.

Slovak broadcast of September 19, 1938.

Andrej Hlinka in Paris.[4]

The problem of the Slovak demand for self-determination is not new.

Slovaks have been trying for twenty years to obtain what the Prague government forcefully denies them, the right to decide their own fate alone and without terror. As early as 1919 the representatives of the Slovak people foresaw that our lot would deteriorate from day to day under Czech rule. The Paris Peace Conference debated the future of Slovakia in 1919 without giving us an opportunity to be heard in spite of the demands of the Slovak people in the Declaration of St. Martin.[5] The Declaration of St. Martin had been arbitrarily altered by Milan Hodza,[6] a tool of the Czech Mafia, but he was powerless to prevent Slovak representatives from going to Paris to try to achieve our national self-determination.

Andrej Hlinka with four of his followers went to the Paris Peace Conference in October 1919. There he protested publicly against the strong-arm methods of the Prague government.

The memorandum our poor leader submitted at the conference contained among other matters this proclamation: "No other people has had a history as full of disappointments as the Slovaks. America was convinced during the war that in the new Czechoslovak state the Czech and the Slovak peoples would live side by side as equal partners. But the agreement (creating the new state) has not been fulfilled, and today those who have usurped political power ignore the question of Slovak independence. Their every effort is bent on creating a Czechoslovak people, an ethnic monstrosity, rather than creating a Czechoslovak state. Thus, instead of gaining our promised freedom, we became victims of a new slavery. Instead of Slovak autonomy, we were subjected to Czech rule. Having rid ourselves of the Hungarian yoke, we came under the Czech yoke which is worse than that of the Hungarians because the new slavemasters pretend to be our brothers.

Slovakia today is a Czech colony and the Czechs treat us accordingly. They destroy all our property. Requisitioning in Slovakia is handled more vigorously than it was ever handled before, even in the World War. Some areas such as the Trencin district are suffering from hunger.

We joined the Czech state in the expectation that we need not fear for the future of our race. This expectation has given way to cruel disappointment because we can now see the intentions of the Czechs clearly - they want to exterminate us. What has not been destroyed by the Magyars in a thousand years is now being taken from us by our Czech brothers. To show the Peace Conference that we are telling the truth, we repeat our demand for a plebiscite in Slovakia. Its verdict will show the true will of the Slovak people. This plebiscite, however, must not be held under Czech terror but under the protection of a neutral military force."

These were the demands of the Slovak representative, our great leader Andrej Hlinka, twenty years ago. And this is what Slovaks are demanding today to safeguard their own future and the peace of Central Europe.

Source: Slovenska Revolucia, pp. 27, 28.

The only comment called for by this rather straightforward account concerns a seemingly unimportant word, the word our "poor" leader in reference to Andrej Hlinka. It will also be seen again in later broadcasts. It is by no means certain whether reference to a man as "poor" is customary when speaking of someone who has recently died, or whether it denotes an element of self-pity which would constitute an important ingredient in the propaganda approach used by Mutnansky. Self-pity is but one step removed from hate for the oppressor who has caused the pitiable conditon.

Slovak broadcast of September 20, 1938.

The important article of Dr. Hletko.[7]

Today's Vienna newspaper *Neue Freie Presse* has published a long article by Dr. Hletko, president of the American Slovak League in Chicago, who recently visited Slovakia with a deputation of the League in order to demand the Prague government's fulfillment of the Pittsburgh Agreement.[8] Dr. Hletko's article confirms the sentiments of all Slovaks at home and abroad when he says: "Our stay in Slovakia has convinced us that the Pittsburgh Agreement has not been remotely fulfilled and that peaceful conditions in Czechoslovakia can only be maintained if the Czechs fulfill all its stipulations. The treaty has not come any closer, after twenty years, to fulfillment than it had at its inception. Without this treaty, however, the Slovak people in America would never have contributed the tremendous sacrifices of money and lives that they offered for their freedom. And without this agreement there would never have been a Czechoslovak state."

Dr. Hletko goes on to say that the Slovaks tried to win the right of self-determination during the World War, but that they have not yet achieved it. The Pittsburgh Agreement played an important role in the creation of the new state, but it was used by the Czechs only to mislead the Peace Conference and to establish their own unlimited control over the Slovaks.

When the Czechs had achieved what they wanted, they were not ashamed to deny the validity of the Pittsburgh Agreement and to have their president declare it to be a fraud. Dr. Hletko called the condition of the Slovaks in Czechoslovakia "much worse than that of the other national groups. The deputation of the American Slovak League studied the situation in Czechoslovakia, and especially in Slovakia, in great detail and came to the conclusion that the present system of exploitation cannot go on. Slovaks must achieve their cultural, economic, and political freedom if they are to govern themselves, rather than being governed by the Czechs." And Hletko continues: "In case of international conflict Slovaks will be forced to pursue a policy designed to safeguard their own interest. But we Slovaks have no enemies in Europe, which cannot be said of the Czechs. We hope that our love for peace will win us the friendship not only of the European nations, but of the entire world. Germany and Italy understand the Slovak problem; thus it would appear that only France opposes its solution by a plebiscite because she is not yet sufficiently aware of the justification of Slovak demands. The sooner France and England recognize the urgency of our problem, the better it will be for the peace of Europe and for European civilization." Thus ends this important article of Dr. Hletko.

Source: Slovenska Revolucia Pp. 17, 18

The favorite propaganda device of using prominent, nonpartisan witnesses in support of one's argument is shown here when Peter Hletko's espousal of the Slovak separatist point of view is reported by Mutnansky to his listeners. While Hletko's prominence may be granted, his nonpartisanship is not. In addition, it is very doubtful how typical his views were of those of Slovaks in the home country. It is fairly certain that the Slovak organizations in America, most of whose adult members left their home country before the birth of the Czechoslovak state, were bound to be less affected by new loyalties engendered by that state than were their countrymen at home. Dr. Hletko thus benefited from what might have appeared to the average listener to be a neutral position, while the group he represented was in reality more likely to take an anti-Czech position than would an equivalent group at home. There can be no doubt that Hletko voices the views of Slovak separatists to perfection and that his position as spokesman of the large and comparatively prosperous group of Slovaks in America must have given special weight to his words to Slovak listeners.

Slovak broadcast of September 21, 1938.

Away from Prague.

The motto "away from Prague" is racing through Slovakia. We do not want to remain associated with people who drive the Slovak nation into misery and extinction.

Men and women of Slovakia! Slovaks all over the world! Watch fearfully what the next hours will bring. We feel that you will hold out and that you will fight courageously against the Judaeo-Bolshevik enemy.

History shows that the Slovak people know how to handle themselves. especially in such hours of crisis; that they are ready, willing to make sacrifices, brave, and, if necessary, ready to die for the freedom and the future of their people.

Source: Slovenska Revolucia, p. 28. Ludovit Mutnansky, Tu rissky vysielac Vieden, p. 38; this book will henceforth be referred to as Tu rissky.

This is the first reference to Judaeo-Bolshevism, a standard National Socialist term linking its arch-enemies. What is remarkable about its use here is that ostensibly the "enemy" against whom Mutnansky would be inveighing are the Czechs; but since it is obviously easier to arouse hatreds against the Jews and Communists than against a brother people with whom one has been living for twenty years, he uses the tactic of first showing that Jews and Czechs have identical interests, and then simply transferring the hatred from the original target, the Czechs, to the more convenient and acceptable one, the Jews.

Slovak broadcast of September 22, 1938.

The whole world is watching with deep sympathy the magnificent struggle of Slovakia for the right of self-determination on the basis of which the peoples of Czechoslovakia are to decide their future by a plebiscite. In these difficult and fateful times it is imperative that the natives of Slovakia maintain a united front. The fate of the Slovak people must be decided by its own free will expressed in a plebiscite.

Sources: Slovenska Revolucia, pp. 28, 30. *Tu rissky,* p. 38.

More clearly than before the demand for a plebiscite for Slovakia is now announced. It will be interesting to note that as the power relationship between Slovakia and Prague shifts in favor of Slovakia after the conclusion of the Munich Agreement, this demand is relegated to the background to be gradually replaced by appeals for outright secession, backed, if need be, by force.

Slovak broadcast of September 25, 1938.
Slovak men and women, brothers and sisters!

Slovaks are everywhere in the front line. We protest that our dear Slovak youths are to be sacrificed for the Judaeo-Bolshevik interests of Moscow's agent Eduard Benes. This is no longer the time for words. Every loyal Slovak must understand the historic hour and his duty.

Slovaks abroad are ready to enter the fight, arms at the ready, to protect the life and property of their brethren under the Tatra Mountains and to free Slovakia.

From Moravia to the Carpatho-Ukraine and from the Tatra Mountains to the Danube the motto must be: to arms, Slovaks, liberate Slovakia long live free and independent Slovakia!

Sources: Slovenska Revolucia, p. 30. *Tu rissky,* p.39.

The feverish excitement of the days immediately preceding the Munich Agreement can be seen from this broadcast which seems to forget all that had been said in the previous days about the need for a plebiscite and demands instead that Slovaks take up arms to fight for their freedom.

The strident tone of the attack against the head of the Czechoslovak state fits into the general atmosphere of the moment.

The readiness of the "Slovaks abroad" to come to the rescue of their brethren requires a word of comment. The broadcast intentionally tried to create the impression that there was a united front of Slovaks all over the world ready to fight against the Czechs. Actually the Vienna Slovaks were the only sizeable Slovak minority that could have been thrown into action. Their numbers certainly did not exceed 10,000 and there is no doubt that of that number a large percentage would have been unwilling to take up arms against the Czechs and would only have done so under extreme pressure of the Nazi regime. It is highly doubtful that Slovak groups outside of Germany would have taken part in any Czech-Slovak conflict.

The broadcast of the following day was devoted to a discourse on the support the late Andrej Hlinka gave to the Slovak separatist Vojtech Tuka. This subject, while of possible interest to the historian, contributes little to the present subject matter. The obvious purpose of the topic was to persuade the listeners that the leader of Slovakia's largest party had been close to Tuka's brand of separatism, which was largely identical with the separatism advocated by Radio Vienna. In addition it was meant to dispel rumors to the effect that Hlinka had fallen out with Tuka and to give support to efforts to obtain Tuka's freedom.

Conclusion

On the basis of the foregoing texts the following may be summarized as earmarks of the pre-Munich broadcasts.

The purpose of the broadcasts was to drive a wedge between Czechs and Slovaks by working for Slovak autonomy within a dual Czech-Slovak state, or to go beyond this to demand outright independence. The demand for a plebiscite to establish the basis for either of these two possibilities played an important role at this time.

The tactical approach used to arouse the separatist (or autonomist) feelings required was based on the following devices:

1. The stress on equating the Czech government with the Judaeo-Bolshevik enemy.

2. An attempt to establish a common front between Germans and Slovaks.

3. A latent, though not as yet clearly identifiable, tendency to use self-pity as an instrument of arousing nationalistic passions.

4. The use of statements by a spokesman of one Slovak-American group to simulate "world backing" for Slovak separatism, and the related idea of making Slovaks at home believe that Slovaks abroad were united in their determination to take action against the Czechs on behalf of their Slovak brethren.

The following chapter will show how these various methods developed during the period following the Munich Agreement.

[1]*Voelkischer Beobachter,* Vienna edition, September 3, 1938, p. 8. The original pretext for the broadcasts was that they were needed to supply accurate information to Vienna's Czech-speaking minority.

[2]Sudeten area is the general term for the German-speaking rim of Czechoslovakia which was later incorporated into the German Reich under the terms of the Munich Agreement.

[3]Historic areas or lands is the term often used to describe the western (Czech) part of Czechoslovakia, consisting of the ancient provinces of Bohemia and Moravia.

[4]Andrej Hlinka was the founder and leader of the Slovak autonomist People's Party which became the leading political group of the nation after the Munich crisis and the state party after independence. Hlinka did not live to see the full prominence of his party having died shortly before, on August 16, 1938.

[5]The Declaration of St. Martin of October 30, 1918 was the work of a group of Slovaks which allegedly contained in its original formulation the limitation of Czech-Slovak partnership to a ten-year trial period.

[6]Milan Hodza, a Slovak, became one of the most prominent Czechoslovak statesmen. Hodza was the nation's premier from 1935 until the period of the Munich crisis. He was the leader of the Slovak wing of the Agrarian Party, an important conservative group in Czechoslovak political life.

[7]Peter P. Hletko was the president of the "Slovenska Liga v. Amerike," an important group of Slovak-Americans.

[8]The Pittsburgh Agreement of May 30, 1918, was an undertaking of Czech and Slovak organizations in the United States to form a united state. Slovaks later felt that the Czechs had not lived up to the treaty's equal rights guarantee to both groups.

[9]Eduard Benes, second president of Czechoslovakia and the most resolute defender of Czech independence against Germany, resigned from the presidency shortly after the conclusion of the Munich Agreement and went into exile. He returned to his native land and resumed the presidency after World War II only to resign again at the time of the Communist coup in 1948. He died shortly thereafter.

CHAPTER VII

THE POST-MUNICH BROADCASTS

While only a few days separate the first of the post-Munich broadcasts from those of the September days, these had been days of tremendous changes in Czechoslovakia as a result of the Munich Agreement concluded on September 30, 1938. The effect of these changes on the country as such were to weaken her military power by depriving her of what had been called her Little Maginot Line in the Sudeten area. In addition, and perhaps more importantly, the refusal of Czechoslovakia's allies to come to her aid against Germany had embittered and weakened Czechoslovak resolve to remain true to her prior political orientation and had started her gradual movement into the German orbit. This change was outwardly symbolized by the resignation of President Benes and the formation of a new government.

In addition to these changes, far-reaching as they were, the very structure of the nation was altered when the Slovaks and the Carpatho- Ukrainians[1] demanded and obtained autonomy status during the early days of October. Thus Czechoslovakia in the course of a few days became a federal state, unsure of herself, uncertain of her future and of her values.

Slovak broadcast of October 24, 1938.

(Note: Mutnansky lists this broadcast as having been made on September 24, 1938. From the facts it contains it is obvious that the date should have been October 24, and the broadcast has therefore been listed under that date.)

The Slovak martyr Professor Vojtech Tuka welcomed home with great enthusiasm.

Sunday there was great celebration in Piestany. The Slovak people welcomed with frenzied enthusiasm its martyr Professor Vojtech Tuka who has at last been freed. Why was he sentenced (to jail) and why did this old man have to suffer?

Professor Tuka was editor-in-chief of *Slovak*[2] and vice president of Hlinka's People's Party. He is really the father of Slovak autonomy and the founder of the Rodobrana.[3] Professor Tuka was and is a scientist of European renown in the field of international law and jurisprudence. In 1928 Professor Tuka wrote an article entitled "Vacuum iuris" for the New Year's edition of *Slovak* in which he pointed out that according to the secret clause of the Declaration of St. Martin a plebiscite was to take place after ten years, i.e., after October 30, 1928, in which the Slovak people were to declare whether they were satisfied with the present governmental system or whether they preferred to change the course of their future.

Professor Tuka maintained correctly that the violation of the Pittsburgh Agreement and of the Declaration of St. Martin (by the Czechs) had created a constitutional vacuum, that is, a situation in which Czech rule over Slovakia was based on power, but not on law, and that non-Slovak holders of public office should be considered no more than an occupying power. The article created a sensation in Slovakian political circles, and reputable Czechoslovak figures like Dr. Milan Ivanka and Dr. Ivan Derer accused Tuka of trying to wreck the Czechoslovak state. The guiding influence in the trial was the super-patriot Dr. Milan Ivanka. With the aid of paid false witnesses they convicted Professor Tuka and sentenced him to fifteen years in prison.

Though completely innocent, the weak old man had to serve almost ten years of his sentence for no other reason than that he was an enemy of the Czech Mafia which had remained in power even after the end of the World War.

Recent political world events have convinced the Slovak public that Tuka's political views have been vindicated all along the line. The Czechs cleverly smeared Professor Tuka's name so that the Slovak people would turn away from him, but they achieved the very opposite. They confiscated the flags and shirts of the Rodobrana, but its spirit lived and flourished. Professor Tuka was released to so-called freedom, in Plzen,[4] but actually remained under close police supervision. At last, on the urgent appeal of the minister of justice, he was set free and went to Piestany.[5]

Professor Tuka was received in Piestany with enormous enthusiasm. The elderly martyr was deeply moved by the way in which the Slovak people welcomed him. In reply to the welcome address he said this: "I shall continue to fight for the rights and the existence of the Slovak people."

We have learned that Professor Tuka remained in Piestany for a short period and has now returned to Slovak political life. He is an elderly man, but both the People's Party and the Slovak government need his ability as scholar and statesman.

All Slovakia greets him with brotherly love and pride and we call out to him in sincerity: Long live the Slovak martyr Professor Dr. Tuka.
Source: Slovenska Revolucia, pp. 21-23.

After a careful start on September 26, the broadcasts now continue what must be seen as a clear effort to publicize Vojtech Tuka, whose separatist leanings, coupled with his pro-German and pro-Fascist views, could not but endear him to the Germans. They preferred him to the clerically oriented center of the Slovak People's Party, made up of Tiso and many others.

Slovak broadcast of October 30, 1938.
What must be done to safeguard the future of Slovakia.

Nobody can protect our beautiful land, our language, our customs, our Tatra Mountains, our beautiful woods, meadows, fields, rivers, water power, and mineral resources better than we can ourselves. We have 100,000 young workers of brain and brawn, and we are the logical entrepreneurs for putting Slovak soil and mineral resources such as iron, gold, silver, copper, cobalt and nickel to such use that our labor will yield golden fruit.

For twenty years we have been waiting for that fruit. Prague has systematically ruined our industry. We have raw material resources under our very feet, but we had to import them so that Jewish international capitalists could spirit abroad and hoard the money they had stolen from us.

As early as the first century A.D. the long since extinct Quadi were mining gold in Banska Stiavnica, and we are still mining it there today. But why are we no longer mining in the Gemerska district, in Dumber, Strba, Ruzomberok, Vychodna, Dubrava, and elsewhere? Because we are told that it does not pay to do so. But today the situation has changed. Today one cannot get raw materials in the world market, and today it would pay to start mining again. This certainly is true of the silver mines, of the rich deposits of antimony between Roznava and Zlata Idka, in Svedlar, near Pezinok and Pernek, which are waiting to be mined; and it is also true of the nickel and cobalt deposits in Dobsina, of mercury deposits in Spisska Nova Ves, in Koterbach, Gelnica, and Zavadka.

We have unfathomable wealth beneath our feet which could have been mined but which was not. The poor Slovak villagers who had no other jobs starved for twenty years because mining did not pay for the Czech and Jewish capitalists. Twenty years it did not pay, but at the beginning of October 1938 it starts to pay again because England magnanimously gives us a loan of forty million pounds which is equivalent to six billion crowns. But, mark my words, fellow Slovaks, she wants as down-payment our ores, gold, silver, cobalt, and nickel. This proves that our mineral resources have a value of six billion and that what was left to us by our forefathers is enough to keep us from poverty.

The whole world has abandoned the Czechs. We have never agreed with their policies, and for twenty years our good Slovak people starved; but today we are to pay for their bills. Never! Slovaks who agree tosuch deals are traitors to their own people.

Do you know that in the Western nations wood is not used for fuel, but that rayon and other chemicals are made from it? Do you know that wood can be impregnated so that it will not burn, but becomes hard as stone? Meanwhile in our forests thousands of carloads of lumber rot away every year that could nourish tens of thousands of Slovaks.

Do you know how the meadows in Switzerland and Holland are cultivated? Do you know that they are treated with artificial fertilizer and produce five times as much hay as ours? That their cows produce ten times as much milk as ours? Look for dairy farms here that are modern enough to build an export industry and you will not find any.

Consider the tremendous losses caused by the lack of flood control. Do you know that if we put the water power of our rivers to good use we would not need to import coal? That our most remote villages could use electric power to plow, sow, cook, heat and light our homes, all of which is still a luxury in our country but an everyday matter in Sweden or in Switzerland? And as for our

Tatra Mountains - their desirable location allows them to compete favorably with Swiss summer and winter resorts.

It is we ourselves who will decide what to do with Slovak resources and wealth. We do not need relations in Prague and godparents in Bohemia. Slovakia belongs to its native people, and it is our people alone who have the right to make decisions and that right is sacred.

We shall build one of the smallest states of Europe. We shall establish close economic ties with the Germans. Germany needs raw materials which we have, and she will help us build our own industrial and economic life.

The Fuehrer and Chancellor Adolf Hitler stated clearly in his speech that he does not wish to have Slavs in his Reich but that he would not stand for subversive neighbors either.[6] Our ministers had the opportunity during their visit[7] to the men who have created the Greater Germany to convince themselves that Slovaks are highly thought of in the Reich. Influential Germans are following with sympathy the political struggle of the Slovak people for independence. In some Slovak political circles the opinion is held that there are several possibilities open to us. If we consider everything thoroughly we must conclude, however, that the only secure future for Slovakia lies in complete independence as a separate state. We must not be frightened and confused. We know of what we are capable. We Slovaks, a crucified people since time immemorial, have never despaired. We shall not despair today either. We put our trust in our Slovak strength and future, and we are confident that soon the sun will rise over a free, independent new Slovak state.

Sources: Slovenska Revolucia, pp. 58-60. *Tu rissky,* pp. 8,9.

The above broadcast gives us a fairly clear insight into several propagandistic methods.

The self-pity motif is now becoming much stronger (crucified people, twenty years' starvation, etc.) and is linked to an equally powerful motif blaming Czech and Jewish "exploiters" and general mismanagement for the economic troubles of Slovakia. In this essentially anticapitalist approach the propaganda resembles modern Marxist propaganda techniques.

Economic thinking has undergone great changes since the 1930's, and it is not surprising that autarchic tendencies abound in the philosophy of the propagandist. It never occurs to him to wonder whether the conditions allowing the resumption of mining in areas that had previously been uncompetitive were not a result of the economic isolationism of the period.

When it comes to the propagandist's attacks against Czech and Jewish economic policies, he distorts the facts almost completely. His listener is bound to get the impression that the Czech part of the nation is gradually syphoning off the economic wealth of Slovakia, whereas every student of the period knows that the true situation was the opposite—Slovaks received heavy Czech financial subsidies. To be sure the mineral wealth of Slovakia, such as it was, did exist and was indeed one of the most important reasons why Hermann Goering, the Reich's heavy industry chief, favored an independent Slovakia long before the rest of the German government. But it was only Germany's economic isolation coupled with the needs of her arms race that made Slovakia interesting to her.

The appeal for complete Slovak separation is becoming clearer than ever in this broadcast and indicates that the autonomy rights granted to Slovakia at the beginning of October, far from pacifying the Vienna propagandists and their Slovak friends, had actually increased their appetite for a complete break with Prague. There is no evidence, however, that this extreme view was shared at this time by any substantial segment of the Slovak people. It may be surmised that the emphasis on Slovak separation was related to the announcement on the same day of German mediation in the Czech- Hungarian border dispute. It is quite likely that the propagandist believed the award to be made by Germany to Hungary of Czechoslovak territory would be influenced in Slovakia's favor by a strong separatist stand taken by Slovaks.

Slovak broadcast of November 22, 1938.
A word about the Slovak racial question.

The famous race expert, Ernst Wagner, has written on the question of the Slavic races and we find the following valuable information in his interesting and educational book.

The Slavic peoples belong to the so-called Dinaric race. This race comprises the following peoples: Slovaks, Serbs, Croats, Slovenes, and Ukrainians.

We must note that the Czechs are not a part of it. This ends the myth that the Slovaks are a branch of the Czech people.

The famous and memorable scientist describes the physical and mental traits of the Slovaks as follows. They are tall, well built, of erect bearing, and their blood is strongly mixed with that of Germanic, i.e., Gothic peoples. Their character is open, honest, virile, cold blooded, steady, warlike, fearless, and faithful. These physical and mental traits are what differentiates the Slovaks from the neighboring peoples that descend neither from the Dinaric nor the Germanic race.

Thus speaks the memorable scientist. The steadfastness and honesty of the Slovak race is proven by the historic fact that the Slovak people, suppressed for centuries, nevertheless preserved their own language, culture, dress, customs, pure family life, and steadfast faith in God. It was for ages and still is the custom in Slovakia that marriages take place only among fellow Slovaks and that mixed marriages are rejected. This age-old custom and other historical discoveries prove that the Slovak people belong to an excellent race and guard scrupulously their purity and identity.

Now that Slovakia is making giant strides in the direction of national independence, it is necessary that we deal with the racial question. A people remains strong and capable only if they maintain their racial purity and avoid mingling with an unequal race.

The Germans have understood and are foremost in demonstrating this lesson, and the Italians, too, are starting to adopt it. The adoption of racial theories does not conflict with religion as the Judaeo-Bolshevik press and Freemason scientists maintain. It is also quite wrong to point out that only Germans and Italians can afford race studies since they are large nations. On the contrary, if these studies are useful for large nations, they are even more so for small nations who depend heavily on maintaining the strengths and abilities of their sons; and it has been shown that racial doctrines are not only of theoretical importance they are of great practical importance in matters of every day existence and economics.

In our new Slovak state we must work in this field, too, and must maintain the purity of the Slovak race to the greatest extent possible. This is a requirement of sound common sense and a necessity for the existence of the Slovak people.

Source: Tu rissky, pp. 10, 11.

Step by step the broadcasts are taking their Slovak listeners down the path to National Socialist ideology. In the case of racism introduced in the above broadcast, one would have expected that the discussion of this subject with non-Germans would offer difficulty for National Socialist propaganda. This, however, was not so, at least in this case where Slovaks were conveniently reminded that Germanic blood coursed through their veins and simultaneously told that they were not directly related to their Czech neighbors.

The broadcast thus illustrates very well the uses to which a pseudo-science can be put when it is manipulated, as was done here, to serve political purposes.

Later broadcasts show, however, that the solidarity of Slavic races was a factor of considerable strength in Slovakia, and great pains were taken to combat Panslavism which, politically speaking, tended to make Slovaks look toward Prague and Moscow rather than toward Berlin for their natural allies.

Slovak broadcast of November 24, 1938.
This is Radio Vienna. We bring news in the Slovak language. The motto of new Slovakia is: To Turn Back is Impossible. We Must March Forward![8]
Zilina: Slovak workers are demanding that Jewish doctors be immediately dismissed from hospitals. It has been found that Jewish doctors are treating Slovak workers with almost inhuman cruelty.
Bratislava: The Slovak News Agency reports two leading officials of the Social Democratic Party have been arrested; they are the Jewish editor Benau and Secretary General Och. They can expect proper punishment. The intellectual leader of the party, Dr. Ivan Derer, does not dare to return to Slovakia from

Prague.[9] We have documentary evidence that for large sums of money Social Democratic functionaries used official cars to help Austrian Jews to escape. Many officials of the Social Democratic Party, such as Schulz and Naci, have managed to escape abroad. We welcome the demise of that party,[10] and we consider the action of the Slovak government a necessity for the safety of new Slovakia. The Slovak public demands that the chief Marxist, Dr. Ivan Derer, also be brought to trial.

Report from Slovakia: The entire Slovak public is highly interested in the questions of working wives of Slovak government employees. From the protest of married Slovak women teachers, published in *Slovenska Pravda,* it can be seen that the teachers are somehow afraid to return to their primary duties, that of being wives and mothers. It does not quite conform to the truth that by losing their positions the financial security of their children and of their marriages is threatened. What is a male teacher to say whose wife does not have an outside job and who has three or four children. Do not complain of being asked to make sacrifices for the autonomous Slovakia. It is a law of nature to live and let live.

The journal of the young Slovak autonomist generation *Nastup* writes as follows: "Professor Tuka—our example. Many who have met Professor Tuka, who is now free again, mention that he has much in common with our immortal leader Andrej Hlinka. This applies both to his mind and to his actions. That is true; Tuka was the right hand of Andrej Hlinka. Professor Tuka loved the Slovak people before and after his arrest with the intensity shared by all patriotic backers of Hlinka. Professor Tuka was unjustly sentenced and imprisoned for ten years. He was the victim of rank injustice. It would be a spokesman of Slovak rights who suffered the worst under the hands of Jewish-Masonic rule. When we greet this great Slovak martyr today, we declare that we shall never cease to follow him. We shall never abandon his program, he is an example to us in everything. He is a Christian in the fullest sense of that word; he is a Slovak, a scholar who for a long time yet will be able to lead and educate Slovak academicians. Tuka has now been rehabilitated, but we do not want to say our final word as yet. Tuka must be given the leadership. He must become the top man in free, independent Slovakia who makes decisions on the basis of his knowledge and of his noble character, and this not only in the university but in Slovak public life as well. Youth will follow him, and so will we all."

The journal continues with another matter dealing with less idealistic aspects. The Slovak papers are full of accounts of Jewish wickedness and of the need for the Jews to emigrate, but at the same time they publish large Jewish advertisements. Can one get everything for money? The same names that we find in the lists of Freemasons can also be found in the advertisement sections of Slovak newspapers.

(The broadcast ended with quotations from the Talmud, the text of which, however, was omitted on the document in the German archives from which this broadcast has been reconstructed.)

Source: Documents of the SD-Leitabschnitt Vienna.

The above broadcast is one of the few whose text in German translation was kept in the German files. It carries the signature of Ludovit Mutnansky, and this would indicate that Mutnansky, while given a fairly large degree of latitude in the selection of material for his broadcasts, also had to take a certain degree of responsibilityfor them vis-a-vis his German masters.

The purpose of the broadcast is by now fairly obvious to the reader. There is the overt anti-Semitism, the linkage of Jews and Socialists, and there is the support given to Dr. Tuka by quoting his backers to the effect that he should take the leadership of the Slovak state. As was said earlier, the reason for this support lies in the fact that Tuka was closer to the separatist tendencies advocated by Vienna than the official leadership of the Slovak People's Party, comprising Tiso and Sidor.

The degree to which the broadcasts interferred in Slovak domestic affairs under the guise of "reporting" was considerable as can be seen from the "people's demand" that Dr. Derer be brought to trial, from the satisfaction expressed over the arrest of the other leaders of the Social Democratic Party, etc. Attention should also be called to the campaign then under way against working wives of government employees. This was a result of the still unmastered economic crisis as well as an indication of the Catholic view on woman's role in society being basically that of a mother, which incidentally for once did not differ too radically from the National Socialist view.

Slovak broadcast of November 25, 1938.

Bratislava: The Slovak government has issued the following communique through the Slovak News Agency: "Our Slovak brethren who have been forced to leave the area occupied by Hungary[11] are coming into Slovakia day after day. They could only save their lives and had to leave behind their property, the product of hard and honest labor. Our brethren are in a totally impoverished condition, and they are physically and mentally exhausted. They are made up of farmers, officials, students, and also artisans and workers. It goes without saying that liberated Slovakia must welcome these brethren of ours and that she must give them housing, food, and clothing. Help our refugee brethren!"

Kezmarok: The German villages of the Zips region[12] have petitioned the state secretary, Deputy Karmasin,[13] to prevent their area from being surrendered to Poland. They state that they have lived in closest friendship with the Slovak people for centuries and want to remain part of Slovakia.

Trnava: We received the following memorable letter. "When we started to clean up our schools and were removing the pictures of Benes,[14] we were embarassed by the children's request 'why not Masaryk.'[15] Supposedly the headmaster had not received any instructions or permission to do so. We, however, know that Masaryk should go even before Benes. We do not want any excepttions; one is like the other. We therefore expect that definite orders will be given to have the pictures of Masaryk removed from schools and public buildings because it is hard to understand seeing pictures of both even in the Ministry of Education. Not Masaryk, but Hlinka, Sidor, and Tuka belong in our schools and public buildings.

Bratislava: Few of the democratic associations of Czechoslovakia were as strongly organized as those of the Freemasons. We are now about to tear the mask from the faces of the secret Masonic lodges that extended their tentacles to all phases of public activity and influenced our leftist domestic and foreign policy and economy. Everybody knows the far-reaching power of the Freemasons whose mysterious rituals are a cover for secret plots hatched in their temples against we Christians. A list of names of leading Freemasons follows.[16] If it is technically feasible we shall also publish the list of remaining Masonic lodges in Slovakia. Let the Slovak people know who its enemies are.

The health of Slovak people should be in the care of Slovak doctors.

From Czechoslovak statistics we can see that for every 12,000 doctors, 1,000 are foreigners. Every country protects itself constantly through new legislation, and we, too, will not permit advantageous gain of foreigners at our expense. Medical circles have drawn attention to the fact years ago that the state spends millions for universities which are flooded up to fifty per cent by foreigners. Our Slovak town of Trnava has only thirteen Slovak doctors plus eight non-Slovak and nineteen Jewish doctors. It is almost unbelievable that the health of the Slovak people even now is in the hands of foreign elements that are hostile to us. The Slovak people demand a final solution to the Jewish question. We have heard plenty of words and want to see action. This is what the Slovaks are saying. You also hear that some people are very much interested in preventing a solution to the Jewish question. In short the Slovak people wait impatiently for a solution to the Jewish question.

Source: Documents of the SD-Leitabschnitt Vienna.

The two first items of the above broadcast must be seen against the background of the Vienna Award of November 2 which gave large segments of Slovakia to Hungary. There was also considerable nervousness at the time regarding Polish claims to Slovak territory. The fact that the German radio station in Vienna quotes demands of members of the German-speaking minority in Slovakia for protection against any cessions of Slovak territory to Poland indicates that Germany after Munich generally opposed such Polish demands.

As has been the case in previous broadcasts, whenever a topic is to be brought up a convenient letter is found as pretext—in this particular case a letter opposing what the Germans called the "Benes spirit" as evidenced by the failure of Slovak authorities to force the removal of portraits of Czechoslovakia's first president from schools and public buildings. Obviously this is another case of direct interference by the broadcasts in Slovak domestic affairs. It is noteworthy that among the Slovak statesmen whose pictures the "letter" recommends as replacement for those of Benes and Masaryk, the name of Prime Minister Tiso is missing, an indication that Tiso did not enjoy the particular support of the Vienna propagandists.

The final item does not even make the pretense of being based on reports from Slovakia, or on letters to the station, and endulges in anti-Masonic and anti-Semitic propaganda. A particularly virulent and almost certainly effective method used is that of holding individuals up to public ostracism by naming and identifying them as Freemasons. The item ends on an ominous note implying that the Germans know or suspect that Slovak government officials are obstructing the implementation of anti-Semitic legislation. As time went on these expressions of "impatience" with leniency demonstrated by the Slovak government in the Jewish question were to grow into one of the dominant themes of the broadcasts, serving the double-edged purpose of spreading an ever more virulent anti-Semitism and of casting doubts on any Slovak officials not ready to do Germany's bidding on this, as well as on any other issue.

Slovak broadcast of November 28, 1938.
News from Slovakia.

Of late certain elements in Slovakia have been arguing that Slovakia is not a viable state under present circumstances, that it has no future, and that it can only save itself by joining its northern or southern neighbors.

It is hard to understand that there are even some serious-minded Slovaks whose sense of nationalism is so "great" that they are willing to lick the boots that have been kicking us for centuries. The Slovak people know well, however, that the Munich Agreement of September 29, 1938, which was a result of the efforts of Chancellor Adolf Hitler, made a great change in the lives of the small nations of Central Europe.

The Munich Agreement and its signatory powers not only guarantee the right of self-determination to individual nations and national groups, but they also prevent any state from treating them like slaves. The times of minority slavery will never return. We Slovaks must understand this and need therefore not bow to anyone, or lick anyone's boots that kicked us mercilessly in the past. Each nation or national group will receive its right to live—the Munich Agreement and its signers, headed by Greater Germany, guarantee that.

It is not necessary for Slovaks to conduct a policy of appeasement; they have not hurt anyone, but have only suffered, and grievously at that.

"God Almighty may allow the Slovak people to suffer, but He will not allow them to perish."

Slovaks have already decided on their political and economic orientation. "Nobody need give us any lessons" say the honest Slovaks. They will never forget the historic truth that we owe our autonomy and the fulfillment of our thousand-year-old dream to have our own country to the energetic support of the German Reich alone. And they also know that neither our northern nor our southern neighbor dared take an inch of Czechoslovak soil until the German chancellor gave them permission to do so. Slovaks know only too well that our northern neighbor, and especially our southern neighbor, need Germany's moral and material support, just as do the Slovaks, and perhaps even more so.

What have they to offer we Slovaks? It is quite clear to all that Slovak political and economic orientation has been decided automatically. And one more thought: New, healthy political principles are growing in Central Europe. They include ethnic rights, new life, new opportunities. We stand at the threshold of a new political and economic era in Central Europe. The era of the Jewish, Marxist, liberalist social order and of feudal parasites has come to an end. No one is stopping it. It is the will of the people that this be so. The victory of the new national and socialist thought is growing apace.

Anyone who tries to resist the avalanche of new national and socialist thought will be crushed. Slovaks want to live in their own independent state as a sovereign people, as equals of other European nations.

Therefore, Slovaks, lift up your heads, tackle your task with confidence. The Almighty will give us the strength to finish the great battle of Andrej Hlinka victoriously.

One people, one party, one happy Slovakia.

Sources: Slovenska Revolucia, pp. 60, 61. *Tu rissky,* pp. 12, 13.

The propaganda appeal of this broadcast is straightforward in its support of a pro-German orientation of Slovakia, and it helps this by appealing to Slovak pride and by inciting old hatreds against its former (Hungarian) oppressors. The argument is clinched by showing Germany as the overwhelming power of Central Europe which fact, the propagandist asserts, makes any orientation other than toward her totally unrealistic. The final slogan reminds and undoubtedly is meant to remind one of the German slogan: One People, One Reich, One Fuehrer.

Slovak broadcast of December 1, 1938.

Professor Tuka was the first man to write about Slovak autonomy on February 5 and 6, 1921. The enemies of the Slovak cause immediately swooped down upon that unusually capable and educated man. The infamous clique (Masaryk-Benes) immediately grasped what was involved and passed out the order to destroy Tuka at any price thus also dealing a devastating blow to

Hlinka's People's Party.

They staged one of the largest and ugliest trials in Czechoslovak history. Black Slovak souls played the role of Judas. The main instigators of the trial were Dr. Milan Ivanka, Dr. Ivan Derer, and Dr. Markovic. Money flowed freely and eye-witnesses were bought who readily testified and swore to everything. To give the proceedings an aura of fairness they appointed an Hungarian, the Communist Freemason Dr. Terebessy,[17] as chairman of the trial judges. But they could not prove anything against Tuka. Nevertheless, on instruction from highest authority, they sentenced Tuka to fifteen years in prison. Professor Tuka was fifty years old when he began his sentence and everybody thought that we would not see him again. And they treated him accordingly.

The political struggle continued.

Tuka was freed and his great dream came true. Slovak autonomy, a Slovak parliament, the Slovak Rodobrana, Slovak military units, all became reality.

Tuka returned home to his fellow Slovaks. It is obvious that Tuka must and will be rehabilitated politically as befits him. He has rendered great service to the Slovak cause, and the Slovak people will never forget him.

Sources: *Slovenska Revolucia,* p. 23. *Tu rissky,* p. 14 (includes two passages not in *Slovenska Revolucia*)   This is a continuation of the Vienna propaganda campaign for Dr. Tuka again under the pretext that they are expressing the will of the Slovak people.

Slovak broadcast of December 4, 1938.

The Slovak proletarian becomes an honest Slovak workman.

We shall have a new Slovakia, a free and independent Slovak state. We are about to build a new Slovakia and new Slovakians. At the same time we must lay down basic principles for the new Slovakians, and we must put relations between Slovaks and Germans, whether in Slovakia or abroad, on a frank and fraternal basis.

It is well known that Judaeo-Bolshevik pressure was systematically applied against the Germans, against National Socialism, and against the Fuehrer Adolf Hitler. This pressure did not emanate only from the Judaeo-Bolsheviks but from others such as the typical democrats who were interested only in their own advantage and not in the welfare of the workers.

Even today Slovaks will be found who preach publicly that National Socialism is dangerous, harmful, and foreign to the Slovak people. It is really typical that those who maintain this have not yet come up with explanations as to why National Socialism is dangerous and harmful. These views are repeated by men who do not even know the principles of National Socialism and who do not know what is going on in Germany. What are the German worker's opportunities?his standard of living? What are his social institutions and laws? In other words, how can one judge without knowing the facts?

One thing is certain and that is that we cannot solve the social problems of the working man by getting him involved in religious doctrine.

Germany cares very little whether its National Socialist legislation is popular or not in Slovakia. But it is natural for us on the threshold of a new Slovakia and of a new life to be ready to learn from others. This is even more true since the institutions and conditions of our neighbor are proven and good. For example, it is the first duty of the citizen in a National Socialist state to work physically or mentally. Every citizen has equal rights and duties. Every worker must have sufficient old-age security. The state is responsible for seeing to it that talented children of poor parents, regardless of the parents' class or job, are given the opportunity of studying at state expense and of rising to the very highest offices. The state is responsible for adequate health of the working population. Child labor is prohibited. A National Socialist slogan states: "He who is ashamed to work is not one of us." And they demand that large enterprises share a part of their net profits with the state.

The German worker is in the true sense of the word a fellow worker in building the state, and his work is of even greater value from an idealistic than from a materialistic point of view. This value can also be seen from the fact that he does not receive a pittance for his work as is the case in the liberal countries, but that the state takes care of the health of its workers. This cannot be accomplished unless the Judaeo-Marxist bacteria which have infected the blood and minds of workers have been thoroughly destroyed. The Jews gained the most from the productive process, but they did not work, they merely traded. You never saw as many Jews behind machines, in mines, or elsewhere as you saw on the stock exchange. The Aryan created value and the Jew took the profit. It is quite natural that National Socialism does not permit parasites on its body. The National Socialist does not know the term "proletarian"; he does not even know the term "bourgeois." These are two enemy classes. The German National Socialist knows only Germans and working Germans at that.

As we can see the basic thoughts underlying German National Socialism are good and sound. We cannot see why these thoughts should be harmful and dangerous for Slovaks. A nationalist must also be a good socialist. He who is not a good socialist cannot be a good nationalist. This principle must be introduced into Slovakia. He who despises, or is ashamed of, a laborer's hands does not belong in the Slovak camp. Slovakia will no longer have proletarians, but only true Slovak workmen.

Sources: Slovenska Revolucia, pp. 39, 40. *Tu rissky,* pp. 15, 16.

One part of this broadcast that deserves special comment is the brief reference to the need for keeping religion out of the social question. It is the first time that this note creeps into a broadcast and shows the basically anti-clerical position of the propagandist. An indirect indication of this attitude may have been suspected earlier in connection with implied opposition to Tiso and his largely pro-clerical group. These suspicions now take clearer form and will become even more obvious in later broadcasts and in other expressions of the propagandists. Obviously, any propaganda effort directed against a country whose pro-clerical leanings were overwhelmingly strong had to be very careful; thus this type of careful remark is of an almost furtive nature.

Slovak broadcast of December 9, 1938.
The capital of Slovakia gives a triumphal welcome to its great son Professor Vojtech Tuka.[18]

We repeat the words Professor Tuka addressed to the Slovak people; "I drew up an autonomy statute and my collaborators were shocked by the fact that it went beyond the Pittsburgh Agreement. I wrote the ill-famed article "Vacuum iuris." What did I accomplish? That Slovaks are no longer content with mere autonomy, that the Slovak people know they are a sovereign people with the right to their own independent life and state. That was my conviction and I told this to the judges who convicted me. I told them: 'I shall accept my punishment with my head held high because I am convinced that my people have the right to their own independent life.' I went (to prison) with my head held high and history has proven me right.

Only those people achieve happiness and territorial security who have their own idependent national existence. They must have their own state, not merely as a matter of right but of duty, the alternative being extinction. We must achieve Slovak independence, not by merely watching what the Slovak government and the Slovak Parliament will achieve; we must all help them."

Slovaks, we shall remember these words well; they are historic words and represent a fact of historic importance.

Trencin: We are informed that Slovak workers demand that Jewish doctors be dismissed from hospitals. They base their demand on the doctors' dereliction of duty and on their inhuman treatment of sick workers.

And here is another important fact—in Slovakia seventy per cent of the doctors are Jews. Frankly speaking, the Slovak workers are saying: "We have no confidence in these Jewish doctors because their religious lawbook, the Talmud, has this to say: Not only the property but the life of non-Jews is given into the hands of the Jews. The non-Jews must be destroyed, particularly the powerful nations. You must kill even the most honest of the heathen! This is what the Talmud says (Aboda Z. 26.2). It is permissable to kill heathen (Chosen 285). And the Jews are obeying their diabolical duties. That is why Slovaks do not want to have anything to do with Jews and demand that the licenses they obtained by such fraudulent methods be revoked."

The Slovaks insist that it is intolerable to have the health of the people depend on Jews without conscience, whose aim it is to destroy the Christian world.

The Slovak people are convinced that the Slovak government will re-examine licenses and will not permit Jews to sell pharmaceutical products. *Sources: Slovenska Revolucia,* pp. 23, 24. (This source does not contain the second half of the broadcast under the heading Trencin.) *Tu rissky,* pp. 17, 18.

The importance of this broadcast lies in the fact that in repeating Dr. Tuka's call for complete Slovak independence, it not only further disseminated that call but also, at least by implication, gave it the support of the German Reich. It will be noticeable from Tuka's final remark about the Slovak government that while he ostensibly asks support for the government, his tone is critical and impatient of the government's moderation.

As for the second half of the broadcast, this is a continuation of the "news" item of November 24, demanding the removal of Jewish doctors from Slovak hospitals. It represents the use of religious anti-Semitism for economic and political purposes. For a comment on the accuracy of Mutnansky's quotations see Chapter II.

Slovak broadcast of December 11, 1938.
We shall not build a happier Slovakia in work camps.

Slovakia is free. Slovak rights have won. The battle which Hlinka's Slovak People's Party waged for almost twenty years has been won. We workers have also participated in that battle and have contributed to its outcome. We are happy about our first victory, and we believe that in free Slovakia we shall also win our fight for a better life.

But these hopes are sadly shaken by the decree of the central government in Prague setting up work camps. We look upon this as something having no place in Slovakia. We shall not build a happier Slovakia in work camps. They remind us of the days of serfdom. We want work, but not under supervision of superfluous officers. If this is what Prague wants, we need not rush to imitate it. Having achieved national independence, we must also maintain our economic independence.

It is a fact that autonomous Slovak workers fought well for Slovak freedom , Slovak bread, and Slovak independence; and it goes without saying that Slovak workers are demanding their share. We understand the ire of Slovak workers, and obviously the question of Slovak bread will not be solved by compulsory labor service and by labor camps.

It is true, on the other hand, that compulsory labor is of great importance, and Slovak workers must try to understand the true purpose and significance of labor service and labor camps. We feel it is our duty to speak briefly about the significance of compulsory labor service. We have heard that this is not properly understood in Slovakia.

The first labor camps were built in Germany. The passionate attacks of the so-called golden world democracies against these labor camps are still in vivid memory. As soon as unemployment started to reach catastrophic proportions, however, and the democrats did not know what to do, they also built labor camps. Their purpose was to use labor camps to do away with unemployment. And this is the source of a misunderstanng also affecting Slovak workers.

The significance of German labor camps and of compulsory labor service lies not primarily in their being a solution to the question of unemployment, but somewhere else, namely in their educational purpose. Compulsory labor service fills the time between school and military service.

In the work camps a young man works without distinction of background,or of future career. He works with pick and shovel, not for pay or advantage, but to serve his people and state.

He spends one year day and night with his comrades doing labor service, and this gives him the opportunity to learn what work is all about. He learns his duty to his nation, and the ideas of honesty, faithfulness, courage, struggle, and leadership are implanted in his mind. Work is the moral basis on which a people can best be unified and strengthened. These basic ways of thinking are best learned by young people in labor camps.

In addition to this, compulsory labor service represents the ideal premilitary training.

Life in the labor camps is planned in every way to meet the wishes of young people. In addition to working, the young men devote their time to education and sports. The camps are constructed simply, but they have everything that is necessary. In short, labor service is a school for life and has been specially designed for youth. The future demands that the new youth be trained in the proper military spirit. Slovak labor camps can be made to serve similar purposes.

In the new Slovakia we must also think of Slovak youth and of educating them in the spirit required by the times.

We know that there are many people in Slovakia who dislike military discipline and spirit. They still have not awakened from the "Schweik" spirit.[19]

Those people are not acceptable in the new Slovakia, and they will either have to change or get out of the way. New Slovakia needs a new youth capable of protecting the independence we struggled so hard to achieve. To achieve this our youth need not only military service but also compulsory labor service.

We are convinced that Slovak workers will understand the significance and the purpose of compulsory labor service and labor camps.

Sources: Slovenska Revolucia, pp. 41-43. *Tu rissky,* pp. 19, 20.

In this broadcast the Vienna propagandists tackled the issue of labor camps which, judging from the heavily defensive introduction, must have been highly distasteful to Slovak workers at the time. Caught between the unpopular Czech imitation of a National Socialist institution and the popularity of that institution among the Nazi leadership, the propagandist createo a distinction between German labor camps and democratic labor camps, the former being educational in nature and therefore valuable, the later being a mere device designed to reduce unemployment and of no deeper value. The implication is that Prague has followed the democratic approach to the problem and that this is why the measure is unpopular in Slovakia. The solution proposed is to have Slovakia form its labor camps on the German pattern which will automatically make for usefulness and popularity.

Slovak broadcast of December 12, 1938.
The Jews are abandoning the Talmud in droves.

A short while ago *Slovak*, official organ of Hlinka's Slovak People's Party, reported that the Jews are running away from the Talmud in droves and that they are trying to join the Catholic or Protestant church.

We have confirmation that a large number of Jews have recently been converted to Christianity. The Slovak public accepts this information with great reluctance. We know well the position taken by Jews toward Christianity, and the Jewish code "Shulchan Aruch" teaches as follows: Every Jew who passes a ruined heathen temple is required to say: "Praised be the Lord who has destroyed this house of idols." When passing a church that is standing he must say: "Praised be the Lord who extends his anger against criminals (read: Christians)."

When he sees 600,000 Jews he must say: "Praised be the Lord full of wisdom"; but when he sees Christians he must say: "Your mother will be exposed to shame and delivered to derision." (Orach Chajim 224.2)

That is the Talmud, a satanic doctrine, and such is the Jew, the devil incarnate. Even if he is baptized, he will act according to the laws of the Talmud; and if he accepts Christianity, he does it only for speculation and for profit.

The following Talmudic utterance is typical; "God perjured Himself when He said that the Jews who had wandered through the desert had no claim to the life to come. Later he regretted the oath and did not keep it. Again when He brought about the reconciliation between Abraham and Sarah, He even lied and that is why it is permissible to lie for the sake of peace and of conciliation." (Baba Meza 87 1).

It is all in vain. A Jew will always remain a Jew. Everyday life confirms that converted Jews are the greatest threat to the Christian world. And it is certain that the Slovak people will not gain the sympathy of their neighbors by the mass conversion of Jews. Quite the opposite. The Slovak people must be particularly watchful now that they are beginning to build their own independent state, that their national and racial purity be protected and that no compromise be made possible on this issue.

The great majority of the Catholic and Protestant clergy opposes the conversion of Jews when it is not a case of spiritual rebirth and genuine contrition but merely a business and a very dirty one at that. The Slovak public expects that the Catholic and Protestant churches will cease all conversions of Jews and will re-examine those conversions that have taken place beginning with September of this year.[20]

Sources: *Slovenska Revolucia,* pp. 5l, 52. *Tu rissky,* pp. 2l, 22.

While undoubtedly the mass conversion of Jews following the events at Munich, if indeed correctly reported, is likely to have been prompted by considerations of expedience rather than by genuine preference for another faith, the broadcast depicts the deep difference between the racial and the religious approach to the Jewish question. The religious point of view would be one that generally tends to treat a human being as a spiritual being with a free will, while the racial point of view treats man as the immutable product of his heredity. There is no question as to the stand taken by the racist propagandists of Radio Vienna. This represents another instance where Vienna took rather sharp issue with the clerical point of view.

A few days before this broadcast the Vienna edition of the official party organ of the National Socialist Party, *Voelkischer Beobachter* had reported in similarly critical terms the attempt by some 1,500 Bratislava Jews to convert to Catholicism.[21] This shows that the problem was receiving close attention by the German authorities, and it also indicates that there was close coordination among the various media in the German propaganda effort directed at Slovakia.

Slovak broadcast of December 17, 1938.

The voice of Slovaks abroad concerning tomorrow's elections.

The Slovak people are approaching the elections to the first independent Slovak parliament. These will be historic elections. It is the first time in the history of the Slovak people that they will choose a parliament that will pass Slovak laws. That parliament will be called to regulate the new Slovak life.

But the significance of Sunday's vents will exceed that of a parliamentary election. They will indicate that the Slovak people declare before the whole world that they intend to live freely and independently in their own country. The eyes of the entire world will be concentrated on the Slovakian elections on Sunday. The world public is still being told that Slovaks cannot live independently and that they want to join a northern or southern neighbor.

On Sunday the Slovak people must give clear evidence that they are not oriented toward their northern or southern neighbors, but that they intend to build their own free and independent life with all the attributes of a sovereign people.

The Slovak people wish to live independently under the Tatra Mountains and within their own state as an equal to the other Central European peoples. Nor is it a matter of who will win the seats in this Slovak parliament, but matter rather that Slovaks will decide on the basis of their right of self-determination if they want to be independent or not.

The Munich Agreement really decided the fate of Central European nations and national groups. The signatories, chief among them Germany and Italy, guaranteed the frontiers of Slovakia as well, and tomorrow it will be primarily a matter of Slovaks showing their determination to live an independent life. In other words, we are speaking of the plebiscite. Every Slovak must understand the great and fateful importance of Sunday's plebiscite.

We know full well that not everything Hlinka's men have fought and suffered for has been accomplished. We know that the list of candidates for the Slovak parliament is not what the Slovak people expected. We know well that the Slovak people are dissatisfied and waiting impatiently for solutions to vital questions. We know, too, that not even in Prague is everything as it should be. This was proved by Wednesday's events in the Prague parliament when Czech deputies attacked the Slovak government and Slovak political institutions in a crude manner. You can see that some people have been unconscious, i.e., have not become aware of the changes that have occurred within the last months, and they have just come to again. They are shocked to see that the Slovak "colony" and the fairy tales about Slovakia are no more. Slovakia has awakened and arisen. To be sure some deep, bloody and painful wounds on our Slovak body have still not healed completely, but in spite of all this, we emphasize again that everything depends on tomorrow. It is part of life that we cannot have everything completely as we wish it, but tomorrow every Slovak man and woman who love their country, with its fields, the Tatra Mountains, the Danube, its language, its people, will vote consciously and conscientiously. Let us not forget tomorrow the years of bitter struggle of Hlinka and the blood and suffering of Slovak martyrs. Let us not forget the future and the fate of our Slovaks abroad which are linked to these elections.

We believe in the victory of Slovak rights and of the Slovak future. We need not fear anyone. We have men in Slovakia today who will fight for our national existence.

As is the leader so is the nation. On Sunday we must give proof of our loyalty to our great leader Andrej Hlinka. Let all go to the polls tomorrow. Go with the deep conviction that Slovaks want to live and will live in their own free and independent country as a sovereign people among the other peoples of Europe.

We swear to you, Andrej Hlinka, that we shall valiantly carry on your great battle to final victory. Slovaks do not forget tomorrow morning everyone votes yes.

Slovak broadcast of December 22, 1938.

Workers' wages in Slovakia are really very low, and the honest struggle of the Christian labor unions for higher wages has been in vain. Owners and managers of firms turned deaf ears to their appeals. When we look for the reason we find it in the fact that almost all leading industrial firms, with a few exceptions like Thybergien in Trencin, were and are in Jewish hands. And the Jews conscientiously keep their Talmudic rules.

It is really interesting to read what the Talmud teaches. The Ten Commandments must only be obeyed toward one's fellow man, that is toward fellow Jews, but man has no duties toward animals. "Thou shalt not oppress the laborer among thy brothers, everyone else is exempt." Cheating a goj (Christian) is permitted. Heathen money is property without an owner and can be taken by whoever wishes to do so. It is always a good thing to take something away from a Christian.

The Talmud teaches all this verbatim. It is a diabolical doctrine, and Slovak workers will now understand why leading industrialists are paying such low wages. Let us just take a look at who the leading industrialists in Slovakia are:

Dynamit-Nobel Co., Bratislava: Oskar Boehm - Jew, Freemason.
Kabelovka, Bratislava: Emil Bondy - Jew, Freemason.
Handl Coal Mines: Hugo Brief - Jew, Freemason.
Schindler & Jedlin, Bratislava: Emil Bluecher - Jew, Freemason.
Karl Stummer Sugar Mills, Trnava: Ernest Goldschmidt - Jew, Freemason.
Zilina Textile Works: Dr. Artur Haas - Jew,
Slovak Alcohol Works, Malacky: Ernst Koenigstein - Jew, Freemason.
Slovak Construction Works, Bratislava: Dezider Krasznyansky - Jew, Freemason.
Diosecky Sugar Works: Oskar Pfeffer - Jew, Freemason.
Slovak Portland Cement Works, Bratislava: Dezider Somogyi - Jew, Freemason.

We could go on like this indefinitely. This is the true situation in Slovak industry. We hear from Slovakia that the workers are demanding that Jews, Freemasons, and their mercenaries be removed at once from their positions.

Jewry, Marxism, and Freemasonry must disappear so that a new, healthy, and happy Slovakia can be born.

Source: Tu rissky, pp. 25, 26.

This broadcast is a continuation of the anti-Semitic line with the propagandists' special predilection in Talmudic quotations and the further refinement of seeking out individuals for personal ostracism. Having been incited, the listener is then told that "the people" (in this case the workers) arc demanding anti-Semitic action.

Slovak broadcast of December 23, 1938.
Protect the children.

At Christmas time every adult likes to think back to the days of his childhood; to the time when the present struggle for a living was not yet as hard and unscrupulous. I am thinking of the time when we believed every word of the miraculous traditions and did not know how much wickedness, evil, and filth there is in this world.

The most beautiful trait of a Christian childhood is its purity of soul. It is childlike and wants to remain so. It is not concerned with adult affairs; they are strange to it, a world of which it does not wish to take cognizance. The Christian child's mind develops slowly as nature wishes it. It rejects everything that is not linked to the stage of its mental development. It rejects particularly impure and immoral speech and habit that contrasts with the purity of childlike feeling and thought.

But how different are Jewish children.

The Jewish child matures earlier in body and mind than the Christian child, and this circumstance has the efect of the child concerning itself with matters that Christian children do not wish to know and understand.

To this something else must be added: Jewish children by heredity and parental environment acquire abnormal and immoral tendencies. Jews have the devil in them, and this devil awakens at an early age. It can be observed primarily in improper speech and habits.

We could show hundreds upon hundreds of examples of immoral behavior of Jewish ten-to twelve-year olds, and these children of the devil spread immoral talk among Christian children and poison the soul of the Christian child in a diabolical manner. We must protect Christian children from that danger. Therefore we must prohibit Jewish children from attending Christian schools, public places like swimming pools, playing fields, etc. We must segregate them. Children, youth that is our golden treasure, the future of our people. We must guard it zealously.

Sources: Slovenska Revolucia, p. 50. *Tu rissky,* p. 27.

The anti-Semitic radio campaign now has reached the medieval level. As in the case of the campaign against Jewish doctors, it was seconded by the German press. The *Voelkischer Beobachter* reported that Bratislava German school children were demanding that Jews be expelled from their school, etc.

Slovak broadcast of December 24, 1938.
The Voice of Slovaks abroad at Christmas time.

Slovaks abroad are spending their Christmas in real and great joy for the first time—the Slovak people have seen the fulfillment of the first part of a thousand-year-old dream. The Slovak Christmas tree is illuminated with Slovak freedom and independence. When we light our Slovak Christmas tree tonight, we will think gratefully of the strong arm of world peace and of the man who made the Central European peoples achieve their long-sought, sacred right of self- determination.

Slovaks beneath the Tatra and those around the world will think with grateful love, with that genuine Slovak love, of Adolf Hitler, the leader of the German nation. Without him and his wholehearted effort our Slovak Christmas tree would be as sad, forlorn, and poor as it has been for centuries upon centuries.

Slovaks understand today that no matter how political events in the Danube Basin and in the East develop in the future, we Slovaks will not lose our importance. This strong conviction heightens our Christmas joy.

Slovaks abroad today, gathered under the Christmas tree, ask the Almighty that their cultural, social, and economic rights in the various foreign countries of their residence may be assured, that an Office for Slovaks Abroad be established, and that they may be able to return to our beloved Tatra.

"O thou whitehaired Tatra
We, thy children are far from thee,
But weep not;
Thy servants
Are keeping faith even beyond the seas."

May the message of peace and tranquility spread all over the world. Peace to those of strong will.

Source: Tu rissky, p. 28.

This Christmas message, so typical of the "Christian" spirit of National Socialism, contains one line of particular political significance mention of the fulfillment of the "first part" of the Slovak dream. It represents the clearest indication yet that the autonomy status accorded to Slovakia during October and November 1938 was not considered sufficient and that the Vienna propaganda line was now aiming for complete independence.

Slovak broadcast of December 25, 1938.

Let us build a new Slovakia.

Let us prepare for a new, better future and for our own Slovak state. We want to be and we shall be a free, capable, and healthy people among the other nations of Central Europe.

The first prerequisite for the achievement of this is the safety of the Slovak people, and the second an increase of the Slovak population.

The renowned Slovakian professor, Dr. Alois Chura, writes as follows in his excellent work *Slovakia Without Progeny:* "At the beginning of this century the Slovak birth rate was favorable. In 1902 the highest growth of the last 35 years was recorded. It dropped sharply in 1915 and 1916 reaching its lowest point in 1918. After the end of the World War the birth rate started to rise again in 1919 and by 1921 the level of 1904 had been regained. It remained on the pre-World War level for three to four years until 1924 and after that year fell off rapidly reaching its bottom in 1935.

"Postwar growth is a usual development after large wars. This physiological development, while fairly pronounced, was not of sufficient duration in Slovakia due to offsetting influences.

"Population growth in Slovakia can be characterized by observing growth in urban and in rural areas. We collected statistics and found that the lowered growth rates applied equally to towns and villages; in other words, they are as prevalent in rural areas as in the cities. This enables us to reach the conclusion that Slovak villages and rural areas are in great danger.

"The weakening of family ties has been greatly influenced by the writings of Marx and Engels (We noted that both were Jews) and by other theoretical and practical propagandists of similar leanings.

"The family is sick. It is in our interest that it be strengthened not weakened. Our population number is greatly affected by the large number of stillborn children. Considering the strong decline of our births, every child that survives is an important factor in the national balance. Abortion, regardless of the method used, has a powerful direct or indirect influence on the decline of the birth rates.

"One-child families: Women are trying to avoid having any children, or to keep the number of children to the minimum. The one-child system is a very unfavorable and even dangerous institution both from the point of view of population growth and from that of social development in a material and, more importantly, in a spiritual sense. The largest number of replies to the question why marriages remained childless was in effect that parents did not wish to to have any children. Western man does not wish to live as a solitary individual, at least not typically. His tragedy lies in the fact that not only does he not care for his forebears, he seems to care even less for descendents who are proud of him.

"A young man (today) does not look for a girl as the mother of his children, but as a mate. The female ideal of our ancestors, however, was a woman who devoted herself to her duty as a mother.

"My words are written in accusation; they will continue and will not be silenced.

"The struggle must be waged against wholesale social disaster, against infant mortality, tuberculosis, inhuman living conditions, alcoholism, venereal disease, cancer, and mental disease, which threaten the present and the future of our people.

"Public care for children is everybody's concern. One must stress that the church does not pay any attention to this important problem. The only guarantee for an improved population policy and for protection of the family lies in the protection of the children in our families. I have pointed out our failures, pain, mistakes, and guilt. May their recognition be a step toward their improvement." So writes Dr. Alois Chura.

At the turn of eras, at the crossroads between East and West, we must be and we wish to be a connecting link. We can succeed if we so will it because the Almighty gave us our historic mission in this part of the world. It is up to us to decide whether we have the will to succeed. The memorable words of Professor

Chura deserve the attention of the entire Slovak public.

We are raising a new Slovakia and a new Slovak man. Every member of our people must learn to understand his duty.

Peace to those of strong will.

Source: Tu rissky, pp. 29, 30.

Speaking of the underlying anti-clericalism of some of the broadcasts, it is of particular importance that the subject of population, which is in this instance treated in a way that is partly analogous to the declared doctrine of the Catholic church in Slovakia and elsewhere, is used nevertheless for an attack against the church accusing it of doing nothing for the care of children. Slovak broadcast of December 30, 1938.

Have Slovak women ever stopped to think why Jewish women do not take jobs as servants, as laundry women, as field hands, as waitresses; or have Slovak men ever thought why Jewish men do not take jobs as servants, farm hands, mountain herdsmen, behind the plow, or as sharecroppers?

At the same time we see that almost every Jew has a female servant and that girl is a Christian. How does he treat her? She must work hard from dawn to dusk to earn a few crowns and, furthermore, she is molested by that Jew. How many thousands of illegitimate children result from this? But the Jew faithfully keeps his Talmudic teachings which say that the Ten Commandments are binding only toward one's fellowman, that is, toward Jews, but they are not binding against wild animals. Not only the property but the life of non- Jews are given into the hands of the Jews. The Sixth and the Tenth Commandments naturally apply only toward Jewish women. Christian women are there to serve the Jews' lust. A strange woman who is not a daughter of Israel is a wild animal. A Jew may go on and on molesting a non-Jewish woman. That is the Talmud—a diabolical doctrine.

And that is why the Jew hires a Christian woman only to abuse her in every way. How many thousands upon thousands of honest Christian servants have been ruined spiritually and physically because of this Jewish deviltry? But the Jews derive the greatest spiritual joy from it, and their religion orders it. But enough has been said about this already, and the Slovak people demand that a law be passed prohibiting Jews from hiring Christian women for their homes.

In new Slovakia every Slovak soul is valuable and necessary. We must not allow the Jews to destroy and soil our Slovak blood. It is the duty of the responsible authorities to free our Christian girls from the claws of Jewish devils. We must also make it possible for our girls to find husbands or, if need be, find other ways of earning their living. But they must be released from the Jewish inferno at once.

Sources: Slovenska Revolucia, pp. 49, 50. *Tu rissky,*

The purported Talmudic quotations are partly identical to those used in the broadcast of December 22.

Slovak broadcast of January 1, 1939.
New Year - new paths - new work.

Slovak nationalism and Slovak Catholicism have been taking a friendly attitude toward German National Socialism.

A few days ago the spiritual leader of the Hlinka Guards, Canon Dr. Karl Koerper, published an important article in *Slovenska Pravda*. The article is of special relevance because it appeared in the official organ of Hlinka's Slovak People's Party and because it was written by an official representative of Slovak Catholicism.

The article reads as follows:

"Our Germans are now living contentedly amongst us. And that is good. You can treat individuals as members of a minority, but not the soul of a people. The Germans are spread out throughout Slovakia. They are a minority, but their new national spirit, as demonstrated in the National Socialist movement, is no longer satisfied with minority treatment, having become basic to German life. And we must respect this and do so gladly.

"Here in our free Slovakia the swastika is as much a symbol of national rebirth and of new life as is the Slovak cross.

"It is necessary at this time to blot out a series of devious erroneous thoughts. There are people who want to talk us into believing that we are now under German influence, that Germans and their ideology are going to make their weight felt around here, that our fate will be a sad one, that after the Jews have been taken care of the church and the priests will be next in line, and finally the Germans will end up suppressing Slovak national life.

"The Germans again are haunted by unfounded rumors that we Slovaks will not tolerate German culture amongst us, that at any moment we are likely to chase them away with gendarmes if they try to live their own national lives, that we want to turn them into Slovaks, etc.

"We can give this reply to those lying spirits:

"We Slovaks are not afraid of the Germans. Modern Germany is the product of national spirit and of strong leadership. Its strength is not so much due to numbers, but to unity and to national cohesion. We have imitated Germany's example. We, too, possess national unity today, and we build our state on the basis of national cohesion. Thus we have reached the same level ethnically and also governmentally and politically that the Germans have reached. And the Germans respect us for that because today a teacher no longer beats his pupil when he sees that he is fully trained and ready to go out into the world on his own.

"Yes, we are under the influence of German culture and political wisdom, and this safeguards our future and our ethnic development. Until now we have been subservient to French Masonic bigwigs and to Jewish capitalism. That subservience killed our ethnic spirit."

Slovak and German circles in Slovakia have welcomed this statement. However, we must not be satisfied with academic statements but must proceed to put our friendship into effect. It is clear that in order to keep in step with our great neighbors we must first of all solve the Jewish question in Slovakia. This we can solve thoroughly only on a racial basis. We know that this cuts deep into living tissue, but we cannot help that. Our people and their future depend on it, and therefore we cannot and must not make any exceptions. We must announce quite clearly that everyone with Jewish blood in his veins is a Jew. This is the only way to keep our people young and fresh, to keep German sympathy, and to guarantee our own future.

In other words, in this new year we are starting on a new political path.

Hail to our immortal leader Andrej Hlinka. Long live our great friend Adolf Hitler.

Sources: Tu rissky, pp. 32, 33. Handakten Seyss-Inquart.

Slovak broadcast of January 2, 1939.

The census of December 31 came as a great surprise to all sections of the population, particularly as the brief notice that preceded it made it impossible for many to be home to take care of personally answering the census questions.[24]

The brief notice and the secrecy surrounding the census until the very last moment were of no special significance for the Slovak people. They were bound, however, to create suspicion among the non-Slovak groups in Slovakia, especially among the German minority which saw itself suddenly confronted by action likely to upset the good relations and perfect cooperation which undoubtedly had so far existed. It is this very fact which seems to us to be highly serious at a time when consolidation, progress, and constructive efforts are called for. Only in frank cooperation that excludes reservations and surprises of the kind that took place on December 31 is there assurance for a happier and better Slovakian future.

State Secretary Karmasin addressed a telegram of protest to Prime Minister Tiso on the day of the census in which he called particular attention to the fact that the German minority refused to accept the census findings regarding its group as binding. In his New Year's message, State Secretary Karmasin emphasized the will of the German minority to go on supporting the reconstruction of the country under the proviso that the governmental policies pursued be open and honest and avoid revivals of tactics from the era we have just overcome. The German minority is ready for cooperation, but also for self- defense.

The method in which the census was taken has met with general displeasure in Germany. The German newspapers, too, stress that a better future can only be built by mutual honest effort. The basic requirements for cooperation are available, they say, and it is now only a matter of frankness. Delaying tactics are utterly useless and would only lead to new difficulties which would delay the recovery of the country.

The *Voelkische Beobachter* writes: "Karmasin protests the Census," while the *Neue Freie Presse* has this to say: "The totally unexpected census in Slovakia has caused general surprise and has been sharply criticized in several quarters. Although the German minority has expressed its full confidence in the government at the time of the last elections, the census was announced suddenly without prior discussion and without notification of the German minority which was thus disregarded entirely." The *Neues Wiener Tagblatt* says: "The census which has been ordered taken on December 31 is likely to upset seriously the previous good relations between the German minority and the Slovak government." The *Wiener Neueste Nachrichten* uses the following headlines: "A Surprise Move in Bratislava," "Secret Measures," "Concern Among Minorities," "Fear of Demonstrations," etc.

It is obvious that this severe setback to the good relations between the Slovak people and the German nation must be removed as quickly as possible. It is expected that the government in Bratislava will clarify this unpleasant matter.

The Slovensky Robotnik writes: "We cannot understand why the non-Slovak and non-Christian labor unions have not yet been liquidated. They share a large part of the responsibility for the actions taken by the Czechs against Slovakia in the course of the last twenty years. Through constant agitation on the part of Czech union officials Slovak workers have been misguided and led into opposition to their own people. This is the major reason why we had to wait so long for autonomy. One would expect that those (Czech) gentlemen have been warned by the events of the last months. That is not so, however. The speculators who lived from the calloused hands of the Slovak workers have not yet learned the new order of things. They still want to "represent" Slovak workers. They refuse to understand that they have ceased to represent anyone and that their membership has abandoned them. They still try to persuade Slovak workers to pay their dues to Prague, but they do nothing to expedite relief payments. They convened an outright anti- Slovak meeting at Brno. That meeting went on yelling against the Slovak unions as if nothing had happened. It is ironic that even today it is a Czech who represents many Slovak Social Democratic unions at the Brno Congress. If those gentlemen from the non- Slovak and non-Christian unions were really concerned with Slovak workers' interests and not solely with their own, they would act quite differently. They would use their influence to see to it that their members are not discriminated against by Prague when they join the (new, state-sponsored) Slovak Workers Union. They would see to it that Prague, which squezed union dues out of Slovak members for years, returns part of that money to Slovakia so that the misguided Slovak workers do not have to wait through the worst part of winter without any relief until the spring."

The following interesting article appeared in the *Nove Piestany* magazine:

"In recent times we witnessed many Jews in Slovakia and in Piestany leaving their religion and converting to the Catholic faith. The large number of Jews, the same Jews who formerly exploited Catholics now converting to Catholicism arouses suspicion. Why do they suddenly seek to be converted? Do you believe they do it out of conviction? The answer is no because if that were so, they would have done so long ago, not now after October 6[25] when we gained our own Slovak government which has declared that it will fight with all its power against the Judaeo-Bolshevists and Jewish Freemasons who have been exploiting Slovakia for twenty years. They convert today because they believe that the government will not persecute them once they are Christians and will not make any changes in their property. The Jews are nearsighted enough to believe that they will be able to continue making their dirty deals at the expense of the Slovak people. But they are very much mistaken. Messrs. Schoenfeld, Gutmann, and Weiss[26] are trying in vain to convert themselves; they will in vain try to put signs in their shop windows announcing that their businesses are Christian. Nobody will believe them. Instead people will point at them and say: "Look at the Jew who converted himself thinking that this would enable him to continue doing business. Our people know very well who exploited and disappointed them for twenty years and the Jews will try in vain to hide behind a baptismal certificate. No one will believe them because every one of us will know that this is the same wheeler-dealer Jew as before. In our new, free Slovakia the hour has come for the Jews, for all the Jews who came here from Poland with a knapsack on their back and who now own millions which they squeezed from the hard work of the hitherto suppressed Slovak people."

In this connection we have been informed that during the last two weeks county offices have been flooded with paperwork connected with the conversion of Jews to the Catolic and Protestant churches. Most of the Jews are big businessmen or representatives of Moravian firms.We have reports that the news about the conversion of Jews is received with indignation by the religious Slovak population and that people are criticizing it publicly. The Slovak people cannot understand the positions taken by the Catholic and Protestant churches in this question. The dissatisfaction of the people is growing daily.

Source: Handskten Seyss-Inquart.

The surprise census taken by the Tiso government affords a good opportunity to test whether the Vienna broadcasts were indeed the voice of the Vienna Slovaks or of all Slovaks abroad, or if they were merely the voice of the German government and its Vienna officials. The conflict involved here was one between Slovak national interests and the interest of the German minority in Slovakia, and predictably Radio Vienna sided squarely with the German minority against the Slovak government, thus answering this question quite conclusively.

The reaction of Radio Vienna and of the German press cited in this broadcast served as a lesson to all those willing to listen to what Slovak "independence" would really be like if any Slovak government ever dared oppose German wishes.

For previous reference to the subject of Jewish conversions see the broadcast of December 12. The anti-clerical position remarked upon in connection with the earlier broadcast is again noticeable, and there are even the unmistakable ominous undertones threatening the clergy with the people's ire.

Slovak broadcast of January 3, 1939.

Bratislava: Today's *Slovak* deals extensively with the Slovak census and states the official views of the Slovak government on this issue.

The main organ of the Deutsche Partei,[27] *Grenzbote,* writes that the question is not so much one of whether the census as such ought to be rejected, but whether the form chosen for it was correct. *Grenzbote* adds that even prominent Slovak political figures received their first news of the census through the radio. It is to the credit of State Secretary Karmasin that the census could be taken without a hitch. Addressing the German minority on the radio on Saturday Karmasin had asked them to do their duty.

In addition everyone is surprised that it was possible for Jews to declare their nationality as being Slovak. This is no way to increase the number of Slovaks. It would be advisable to add State Secretary Karmasin to the Cabinet to avoid similar misunderstandings and distrust in the future.

The new Slovak life must move along the same lines as the German and Italian revolutions. We Slovaks must acquire the spirit of the German revolution for only in that way will we successfully finish the work of the revolution of October.[28]

The *Grenzbote* of January 3 writes as follows: "On Monday evening, Ing. Muehlberger, the representative of German unions in Slovakia, called a meeting of union representatives of the German workers of Bratislava at the union offices of the Deutsche Partei to discuss the plans of the Slovak government to form a state-sponsored union. The meeting, which was addrssed by - amongst others - the minority leader State Secretary Karmasin, who gave a survey of the present political situation, reached unanimous agreement that German workers having old union traditions will organize only in an existing separate German union. The minority leader expressed the hope that the Slovak government would keep its promise to grant full freedom and independence to the German minority in this, as well as in all other phases of activity, since the Germans in Slovakia would rather use their strength for constructive effort than for national struggle."

We have just been informed that a five-member deputation of the American Slovak League will come to Bratislava for the first session of the Slovak parliament on January 18. The popular writer, Konstantin Culen, will leave for America after the first session of the Slovak parliament.

The Slovak deputy Jozef Srobar[29] writes as follows in *Slovak:* "Work and modesty will be our future guidelines. The new leadership succeeding Andrej Hlinka is following these guidelines and is working to the utmost of its ability. I do not know whether they have had a moment of rest or a restful night since October 6; and I believe that this situation will continue for a long time to come because when it comes to hard work, these new men will be the faithful heirs of our immortal leader Andrej Hlinka. I spoke with Minister Karol Sidor a few days ago. He told me that he was given a very luxurious four-room apartment in the Prague ministry where his office is located,but that he did not feel comfortable there since the surroundings were strange to him. To lessen the luxury he had a cross mounted on one of the walls.He also mentioned that his apartment was still furnished as modestly as when he was a simple citizen. All this proves that the Slovaks are trying to imitate their leader Andrej Hlinka's modesty and that they are not becoming 'lords' since that is expensive and money is something they do not have. Modesty must become our motto and must remain so while we go about taking care of our ethnic and political obligations. We cannot afford to do what great nations do; we cannot imitate them because that would be our ruin. We must begin by lifting living standards among the poorest; the others can wait. In everything we must look out for the people's interest and not for that of the individual. We must act in accordance with Andrej Hlink's guidelines whether this be in the field of education, politics, or economics."

According to news reaching us from Bratislava, Minister Karol Sidor is opening a course for Hlinka Guard officers. The course will start today for those officers sent by the army command to train with the Hlinka Guards. It will begin with a public meeting and with a speech by Karol Sidor, commander in chief of the Hlinka Guards, and will last from January 3 to January 5. Lectures will be given by Dr. Vojtech Tuka, Karl Murgas, chief of the (Guard's) political staff, by Colonels of the Reserve Cunderlik and Pulanich, by Captain Dualsky, by the chief of the economic department, Jan Horacek, and by the chief of the legal department, Dr. Jan Durcansky. Sixty officers will participate.

The following official announcement has been received from Bratislava: The government has ordered the Union of Private and Public Officials of the Czechoslovak Republic to be dissolved in Slovakia. The dissolution remains in effect until illegal activities of the union have been clarified. On the basis of this order the police of Bratislava have confiscated all the property and correspondence of the union and have started an investigation into it. Local police in other areas of Slovakia are taking identical action against local chapters of the union.

A letter containing the following has reached us from Stupava: The Jew Rosenthal owns a grocery store common for Slovak Jews. The Hlinka Guards issued an order to watch persons buying in Jewish stores. Thus, two young men who call themselves Hlinka Guards were put in front of Rosenthal's store. Some time later we observed that the Jew Rosenthal called the two Guardists into the store and discussed something with them in typically Jewish manner whereupon the two young men disappeared. A while later the Jew stepped outside his store and happily told the gentlemen who had observed the incident: "You can buy here again without restriction."

It will be necessary for the leading men of the Hlinka Guards to pay more attention to the question of who joins the party and the Hlinka Guards.

Source: Handakten Seyss-Inquart.

The clever way in which Karmasin and the German minority in Slovakia replied to Tiso's census move by raising new demands and lacing these with fairly open threats is noteworthy. As was mentioned earlier, Tiso was forced to give in to the demands, and the census incident actually ended with the German minority in Slovakia more strongly entrenched than before.

The curious use of the word revolution by the Slovak-speaking Vienna radio propagandists to describe events such as the Zilina demand for Slovak autonomy shows their predilection for revolution as such. It is noteworthy that this word would hardly have been used by German National Socialists to describe their own takeover of power since in their eyes the word had a leftist connotation.

The final anti-Semitic item in the broadcast again shows the effect that naming of persons or localities has in ostracizing political opponents or, in this case, of seeing to it that Slovak anti-Semites were forced to adopt much harsher methods.

Slovak broadcast of January 4, 1939.
We received the following letters from our listeners:
Bratislava: "The latest Jewish swindle. The journal of the young Slovak autonomists *Nastup* writes very sharply against the Jews. But the Jews know how to help themselves. As soon as *Nastup* appears they buy the entire batch so that it is impossible to obtain a single copy at newsstands. Here the Jews can afford to do this, but they cannot buy Radio Vienna and there you open the eyes of the Slovak public and fight against the Jews without compromise. Keep up the good fight; the Slovak people are grateful to you."
Risnovce: "The women of Risnovce send all best wishes to the Fuehrer and Chancellor Adolf Hitler who supported our Slovak victory. We are loyal to the

Slovak government and to the great Fuehrer Adolf Hitler. We listen to your broadcasts daily with great interest and we wait for the new Slovakia without Jews."

Vrbove: "We listen to your good Slovak news service daily, and we are grateful to the German authorities for organizing these Slovak broadcasts which enable us to get objective news. May the Almighty grant good luck and health to the great Fuehrer Adolf Hitler."

Malacky: "We listen to your Slovak news daily. Everything is happening just as you say it will. You ask us not to buy in Jewish stores and we do not, but there are still many deluded people who do. They should have tags put on their chest and back saying that they are traitors to the Slovak people. We have convinced ourselves that you report the Slovak truth and we are grateful to you. We shall go with Sidor against the Jews. The Women of Malacky."

Nadas: "I should like to remind you of the memorable meeting in Trnava in 1927 when the Jewish-Bolshevik mob stoned and bloodied our late leader Andrej Hlinka. The county president, Dr. Drblohav, was present, and it was he who was the real originator of the bloody incident. We feel that men of his type should be made to leave Slovakia; nothing should remind us of them anymore. The Slovak people will have their reckoning with all enemies sooner or later; otherwise all the anti-Slovak bacilli will gradually return to life. That is why they must be done away with."

Bratislava: The health of the Slovak soldier is a sacred matter to us. That is why we are interested in who takes care of medical treatment for Slovak soldiers. We note with alarm that they are still under the care of Jewish doctors. The commandant of the Bratislava military hospital, for example, is Colonel Friedrich Hahn, a Jew, and the head of the bacteriological institute is the Jewish major Paul Fantl. This situation is intolerable.

We know that Jews adhere to the diabolical Talmudic doctrines and will never treat our Slovaks properly. The Talmud teaches that not only the property but the life of non-Jews is given into the hands of the Jews. Unbelievers must be done away with, especially the important ones. The best of the heathen are to be done away with—that is what the Talmud teaches. Jews are allowed to kill non-Jews.

These Jewish prinicples are satanic. The Jew is Satan incarnate. The health of our boys cannot be entrusted to such devils. There are considerable numbers of well-trained Slovak doctors available. Slovak soldiers ask emphatically that Jews be no longer permitted to serve in military hospitals. The health of Slovak soldiers must be entrusted to Christian and Slovak hands.

Bratislava: The course for officers assigned to the Hlinka Guards started yesterday. It was opened by the leader of the Hlinka Guards and Minister Karol Sidor who remarked that the Hlinka Guards are the political army of the Slovak people.

Source: Handakten Seyss-Inquart.

Slovak broadcast of January 5, 1939.

Bratislava: It has always been a national tragedy of many Slovaks that they wished to serve—whether it be Turks, Magyars, Poles, or Prague. And the worse off our people were, the more those men with slave mentalities would come forward to harm their nation. This is still so today. In other words we are unable to build a solid base for our foreign policy orientation. We have not learned enough from past mistakes, and today we are heading in a dangerous direction. In our New Year's broadcast we read the remarkable article of Canon Koerper who expressed a clear preference for a pro-German orientation. He said verbatim: "Here in our free Slovakia the swastika is as much a symbol of national rebirth and of new life as is the Slovak cross. Yes, we are under the influence of German culture and political wisdom, and this safeguards our future and our ethnic development."

The Slovak people have noted this statement of the representative of Slovak Catholicism with satisfaction and have expected that at last closer cooperation would come about. But the very opposite happened. The census and the manner in which it was conducted left a very unfavorable impression in the German minority in Slovakia and on the Germans in the Reich. To this must be added the fact that a number of firms have dismissed Germans without explanation. These are matters that can have unfavorable effects on the future. It is clear that the latest political developments are the work of the political underworld and have been plotted carefully. The purpose is quite clear to make friendly, good-neighbor relations impossible at all costs. Behind it all are the Jews. The Jews are interested in weakening German-Slovak friendship. Also, there are still people in Slovakia who maintain that the Jewish question cannot be subjected to a radical solution because this would put us under German influence. The cooperation of those people with Jews and other dark powers may yet bring forth very bitter fruit. They mean nothing other than our Slovak people should remain the slaves of international Jewry and not become Germany's friends. Brothers and sisters, think this through while there is still time, and do not let anyone mislead you who is interested only in himself and not in the future of the Slovak people. Political developments in Europe have not yet ended. Those who today work against German-Slovak friendship have the task of forcing the Slovak people back under a foreign yoke. These Slovak pirates have already made their preparations. It is now up to the Slovak people to agree to these tactics or to demonstrate their will to maintain Slovakia's future and independence. Be on your guard.

Bratislava: A large number of Slovaks are working in various German cities. Six hundred of them who work in Hanover and four hundred who work in Berchtesgaden came home for Christmas. In line with German law they received a paid vacation and had their trip paid for as well. It is significant that

Slovak workers in Germany could send home a total of 130,000 crowns after a relatively short time. Within the next few days another series of workers' trains will leave Slovakia for Germany. Seventy-five workers are headed for Osnabrueck, two hundred for the Hermann-Goering works at Braunschweig, and one hundred for Weimar to work on a special project of the Fuehrer.

Slovak workers demand honest wages for honest work and that is right, that is how it should be. But what do we see? Slovak wages are almost the lowest in all of Central Europe.

These last twenty years Slovak workers and their families had to suffer indescribably. Their living conditions were far below sufficiency. Nothing helped. The employers, for the most part Jews, turned deaf ears to their pleas and did nothing to recognize the hunger and deprivations of the Slovak workers. The insufficient social institutions did not react to the Slovak cry for help. All were unwilling to listen and looked at the hunger of Slovak workers with equanimity.

Lockouts and strikes ended in an even greater debacle and the workers paid for everything in cruel ways.

We asked our conscience why it was the worker who had to take great loss when, on the other side, the employer was making giant profits. The reason was that the employer was a Jew who stuck faithfully to his diabolical Talmudic doctrines: You will not oppress your working brethren. All others are exempt from this law. You are permitted to rob a gentile! You may cheat a gentile! It is always correct to take something away from a Christian.

Other reasons were that the Jew was politically powerful, that Christians always helped the Jews to rob their brethren, that officials, political bosses, newspapers, in short, everybody helped the Jews. Behind them was the capital of the diabolical Jewish magnates. They directed, set the tone, and decided on the living conditions of Slovak workers.

After October 6 the sun rose on Slovak independence and freedom under the Tatra Mountains.

Many of our honest workers gave a sigh of relief. They thought the sun would shine on them too. They thought that now they would be able to buy more bread, bacon, meat, better clothes, and be able to spend more on their children, and they were right in believing so. But what has happened?

Let us read the last issue of *Slovensky Robotnik*. The struggle for a bonus for Christmas, for New Year's, and for higher wages is as hard as ever. Why? Because the power of the Jews in Slovakia is just as great as before. The political constellation has changed, and governmental controls have come into Slovak hands; but the most important aspect of life, economic activity and capital, remain in the hands of the Jews. The Jew continues to be the master, and with his capital he continues to rule mercilessly, whether we like it or not.

It is high time the Slovak workers started to understand the Jewish problem and that it is not enough to exclaim "the worker deserves his wages,"[31] or to make speeches about beautiful and lofty but obsolete doctrines which do not improve the workers' lot. We can only assure the Slovak worker a better life if a radical solution to the Jewish problem is adopted. The Jewish problem must be solved by hard and uncompromising methods. It must be clearly stated that Jews are all those in whose veins there runs Jewish blood and that the property of Jews is the property of the Slovak people.

There are some gentlemen who say this cannot be done in Slovakia. That is not true. If it could be done in Germany and in Italy, why should it not be equally possible in Slovakia?

Whoever brings up such arguments has been bought by the Jews, serves world Jewry, and is just as dangerous for the Slovak people as the Jews themselves.

Slovak workers are convinced the Slovak parliament will solve the Jewish problem in accordance with their wishes. Slovak workers are more aware and on their guard today as to what can be achieved and what can not. They are not going to be deceived. That is why they will be on their guard.

Sources: Slovenska Revolucia, p. 47 (contains only that part of the broadcast preceding the paragraph starting with "After October"). *Tu rissky,* pp. 34, 35.

The attack against Slovak servility at the beginning of this broadcast represents a tactic that could easily have backfired since the propagandist obviously is asking for greater servility toward Germany.

The insinuation that it is the Jews who are responsible for Tiso's census is of course a highly clever propagandistic move, the results of which must have been (1) to force Tiso onto the defensive, (2) to deprive him of at least part of his popular support, and (3) to confuse matters by making it appear that it was not really a Slovak- German issue but a Slovak-Jewish issue.

All of these may have contributed to the erosion of Tiso's will to resist the German pressure to which reference was made earlier.

The statement "Political developments in Europe have not yet ended" is an oblique way of using German power as a threat. It was used again in the broadcast of January 9.

The radical tenor of the anti-Semitic campaign waged by Vienna is by now unmistakably clear. The workers' self-pity, to which an appeal had continuously been made, now gives way more and more to the call for action and for the first time the idea that the Jews' property belongs by right to the Slovak people (with all that implies) is clearly stated. Just as the radicalism becomes more pronounced so does the racial aspect of anti-Semitism, with the repetition of the racial rather than religious definition of what constitutes a Jew. This was first mentioned in the New Year's broadcast. Further indication of the radical nature of the broadcast is the statement that anyone who opposes the solution demanded has been bought by the Jews; he is therefore as dangerous as they are and hence ought to be treated like them. Threats are mingled with the hate campaign, and the broadcast ends on the ominous note that Slovak workers expect parliament to adopt radical measures and that they will be watching to see that such are indeed adopted.

Slovak broadcast of January 6, 1939.

Palo Carnogursky recently wrote an article in *Slovak* entitled "Memories" which contained the following lines: "In the second half of September, events were moving at breakneck speed; there were the beginnings of anarchy. Elements ascended from the underworld to suck the people's blood. In Bratislava the demand was raised, in hushed tones at first but later loud and clear, that Sidor be hanged. This slogan came from the underworld in which Sidor's enemies were waiting. They thought their time had come. Hooked noses appeared and the words were uttered from non-Slovak mouths.

"Sidor took it with a smile. To those of us who met in those turbulent days and who hardly let him out of our sight, he said with insouciance: 'They want to break into my home and I have never yet had a revolver in my hand. But I am not afraid and I shall not run away.' He lit a cigarette and looked down on the city with his penetrating black eyes watching the hospital where excitement and panic were constantly increasing. He did not have much time for observation because the telephone was ringing shrilly every few minutes. From all directions people were turning to him in confusion and desperation. In the excitement they did not really know what they wanted of him, but one theme reoccurred in everything that was said: 'Save our people; their fate is in your hands.' There were ever more eyes turning to him. Even at the peak of the turbulence when everything collapsed Sidor remained the hope of those in whose veins flowed Slovak blood but who were prevented by orders from participating in the national effort. In those terrible hours their eyes turned to him.

"And it was during those very worst times that we had to fear for his life. We suggested to him to spend every night somewhere else outside Bratislava. He refused. His faith in himself and in the protection of the Almighty were immovable. He showed himself to be a leader whose only protection was his clear conscience and his willingness to offer even the gratest sacrifice."

In recent times the Slovak press has been devoting much space to economic problems, which are of paramount importance for the new Slovakia. Economics minister Pavel Teplansky writes as follows in *Venkov:*

"My chief duty as economics minister will be to promote the entrepreneurial spirit in the commercial, industrial, and artisan fields in order to expand them and also to introduce a proper proportion of Slovaks into those branches of business in which there are today very few of them. We shall have to educate Slovaks to become good entrepreneurs. In the past our schools have made us into a people of writers and officials. This must be changed since we cannot go on overproducing petty officials. Slovakia within its smaller borders will need many entrepreneurs to turn raw materials into semi-finished and finished goods. She will need many businessmen capable of opening up foreign markets not only for our raw materials and minerals, for the products of our large and small industries, but also for the products of our home industries which must be given new sales opportunities. This entrepreneurial spirit must not only be imbued in that section of our youth which heretofore entered careers as officials or as clerical help, but also in our farm youth since our farmers have not yet progressed beyond the production of primary materials. Under all circumstances we must train our farm youth so that at least sons of numerous families will go into industries using agricultural raw materials as their base, industries such as sugar refining, alcohol production, etc. In our rural areas there are many entrepreneurial opportunities based on the soil, that is on raw materials derived from the soil (our forests, building materials, brick construction, etc.) These products can then be sold again in rural areas. In the past this production and distribution system was in the hands of people who were complete strangers to the farmers. We cannot go on watching small acreages and small farms being subdivided even more. Rather we must re-educate our farm youth so that they can find new ways of earning a living.

"The Slovak government knows well the needs of our rural population just as it knows the needs of our industry, of our commercial firms, artisans, and other branches of our national economy. Several measures are being taken such as the formation of farmers' organizations, the reorganization of the forest and lumber industry, the centralization of artisan establishments, and of finance, as well as other far-reaching measures whose collective effect will be an extraordinarily healthy one. Slovakia possesses many unused opportunities and favorable conditions for healthy enterprises that have so far been hardly touched."

Minister Teplansky's views and plans deserve full approval. It is necessary to add, however, that in the present stage of Slovak economic life the entrepreneurial spirit by itself will be of no avail. There are many examples of young, capable entrepreneurs with capital at their disposal who started work with great enthusiasm. Immediately, however, the Jewish competition, seeing a Christian rival, would pounce upon him. In such cases Jews will sacrifice anything to get rid of the Christian entrepreneur. As a result the Christian entrepreneur could not keep up with his competitors. Jewish competition in the Slovak economy cannot be overcome. The Jews will use their capital strength to destroy any competitor, and as long as economic power in Slovakia is concentrated in the hands of the Jews the entrepreneurial spirit will not help us. And another question: There are many capable Slovak businessmen with means of their own who live abroad. Try to ask them if they would be willing to invest in Slovakia under the present circumstances. Every one of them will decline for the simple reason that the Jews hold too much power in the Slovak economy. Our foreign Slovaks would invest and work.[32] These are facts that cannot be silenced by any theory. If we want a Slovak economy, if we want that commercial activity in Slovakia be primarily in Christian and Slovak hands, then we must first solve the Jewish problem in a radical manner. Jewish businesses should have been put under the control of economic commissars long ago. They should next be gradually Aryanized and put into Christian and Slovak hands.

If that were done Slovaks abroad would also invest with joy and would show their entrepreneurial spirit. But as long as Jews remain masters of the Slovak economy, the question of entrepreneurial spirit is an academic one. We must do more real and tangible work.

Source: Handakten Seyss-Inquart.

The first part of the above broadcast continues the build-up for Karol Sidor which started January 3. This support for Sidor by the Vienna radio was to be short-lived.[33] Sidor's courage, however, was to be demonstrated when he faced a select group of Hitler's bullies during the March crisis and refused to surrender to their demands. It would not be amiss to connect Vienna's obvious displeasure with Tiso over the census incident with this sudden build-up of Karol Sidor.

The final part of the broadcast is built on economic anti- Semitism, and Vienna's proposed solutions are the importation into Slovakia of the economic anti-Semitic measures that had been applied with great "success" in the Reich. The person of Pavel Teplansky was at the time of this broadcast not yet controversial. He was to become so during the March crisis. (See Durcansky's broadcast of March 10, 1939). Teplansky was one of the few pro- Czech members of the Tiso government.

Slovak broadcast of January 7, 1939.
Bratislava: This morning a special commission met to discuss the events in Munkacs and to deliberate on what action is to be taken concerning these incidents.[34] Slovak political circles report that the Slovak and Carpatho-Ukrainian governments are planning to request an arbitration agreement.

Slovak of January 6 writes as follows: "In Bohemia and Moravia Slovak workers are being discharged. The editor received the following letter from a Slovak worker. 'My heart beats faster when I hear of the suffering of our brethren in the occupied zone.[35] But those are not the only Slovaks who suffer; we who work in Bohemia and Moravia are undergoing similar tribulations. After the changes which took place in Slovakia the situation for Slovaks in Moravia also changed. I was employed at the firm of Wilhelm Brothers in Prostejov. At the time of mobilization I went into the service in Moravia. When I returned to my work in Prostejov and went into the office of the manager, Stanislav Kolous, he said to me: Heavens, what are you doing to our people in Slovakia? We cannot give any preference to Slovaks and from today we have no work for you. You can go. We have heard that the competent Slovak officials are highly indignant and that this treatment of Slovak workers in the historic lands will find a similar echo in Slovakia."'

Bratislava: The Slovak News Agency reports that on Thursday a delegation of Jews under the leadership of Dr. Liebl visited the chairman of the Slovak government Dr. Tiso and Propaganda Chief Mach.

The delegation referred to the strong anti-Semitic sentiments in Slovakia and asked the chairman of the government to protect the Jews and to put an end to all anti-Semitic measures.

The visit of the Jewish delegation to the prime minister's office has naturally caused great interest among the entire Slovak population.

Bratislava: We have learned of an incident that deserves the attention not only of the public but also of the governmental authorities. It is well known that Jews are trying to get their money out of the country, mostly, of course, by illegal methods. They are succeeding in this fraudulent activity with the aid of unscrupulous non-Slovak businessmen.

This specific case involves the non-Slovak importers and businessmen Paul Pribula and K. V. Linhardt. Both businessmen import fruit from Hungary, Yugoslavia, and Rumania. A Polish Jew from Brno, Leon Blumenfeld, serves as intermediary for these deals. The firms pay between 4,000 and 5,000 crowns for each carload of fruit. The money goes to Hungary, Yugoslavia, and Rumania where it is again received by Jews. Nobody has been paying any attention to this, and, assuming that about 2,000 to 3,000 carloads are traded each year, the Jews can smuggle out more than two and a half million crowns annually.

It is clear that Jewish exporters are concentrating on these firms and that honest Slovak merchants go empty-handed. There is great need for a thorough house-cleaning in the Slovak economy. The Slovak government needs honest and courageous businessmen.

Slovenska Sloboda in Presov relates the following interesting information. In Sobrance 82 of 120 businessmen are Jews. There are thirty-seven stores of which only three are Christian and Slovak. More than half of all Jewish firms have foreign names. The sales outlet of the Slovenka is in Jewish hands. The manager of the branch office of the Donaubank is the Jew Rado who makes no secret of his hatred for Slovaks. The Jewess Sarah Rado, wife of the man just referred to, owns the only drugstore. The baths of Sobrance are owned by four Jews from Uzhorod. During the last season there was one single Slovak Christian woman employed in the baths, and she too was discharged by the Jew Jakubowitsch. Of the six inns in Sobrance, five are owned by Jews Milder, Schwarz, Winkler, Neumann, and Gutmann. The only pharmacy is run by the

Jewess Sarah Horowitz whose official place of residence is Munkacs, Hungary.
Of the four lawyers, three are Jews. The road taxes and the public weighing station are handled by the Jews Keller and Schoenberger. The secretary of the district artisan cooperative is the Jew Ludwig Rosenfeld who treats Slovaks rudely.
The Jewish butcher Gruenberger has a monopoly on supplying the military.
The Jew Jakob Klein has the franchise for the sale of gas masks. And the only
bakery is owned by the Jews Gruenfeld and Gutmann. This is why on Saturday
it is impossible to get freshly baked goods in Sobrance because of the Jewish
Sabbath.

The Guardists from Budkovce inquire why one of their town officials is still
a Jew while the other three are socialists who support the Jew. They buy only in
Jewish stores and put obstacles in the way of Christian businessmen. The Jews
in the town speak only Hungarian, but otherwise consider themselves Slovaks.
The tobacco monopoly and its adjacent store are in Jewish hands. We ask why
could not the tobacconist at least be a Slovak. The Budkovce Guardists believe
that this situation, which is impeding progress, will be acted upon by the top
authorities.

Source: Handakten Seyss-Inquart.

The item reported by *Slovak* is one of several during that period which
served the obvious purpose of fanning animosities between Czechs and
Slovaks.

The item from *Slovenska Sloboda,* while depicting a situation of almost complete Jewish economic domination of the Sobrance area, fails to supply highly
relevant information about nationality distribution in the area in question. If,
as is likely, there was a high percentage of Jews living there, this would throw a
different light on the situation.

Slovak broadcast of January 9, 1939.
The most acute Slovak problem is the Jewish question.

The fact that the Jewish question has become a world problem is an indication that it must be solved.

In solving the Jewish question in Slovakia we must not forget that no country, or people, has suffered as much under the Jews as Slovakia. The Jews alone
are to blame for our misery and impoverishment today. We still remember how
thousands of honest Slovak families had to leave their homes, and we have not
forgotten the diabolical methods employed by the Jews to exact usury from the
Slovaks.

But the most important thing is that new Slovakia wishes to become part of a
new, healthy European organism, and let us not forget that political
developments in Central Europe have not yet ended.

Today the Slovak people know and understand that the Jewish problem must be solved in theory and in practice in order to free our national body from that dangerous cancer which is devouring it slowly but surely. Compromises and optical solutions can only bring catastrophic results in the future. It is a fact that the Jewish question is closely linked to the future of the Slovak people and that is why it must be decided by the hardest Slovak political logic.

The Slovak people demand that the Jewish question in Slovakia be solved along the following lines:

Point 1:

A revision of civic rights enjoyed by Jews in Slovakia.

Point 2:

A census and registration of Jewish property in Slovakia.

Point 3:

A special property tax on Jewish property to be levied to compensate for twenty years of exploitation of the Slovak people.

Point 4:

Institution of rigorous controls over businesses in Slovakia and appointment of government inspectors for the food business. Thus the Slovak government could give jobs to at least 20,000 people and could reward those Slovaks who suffered for their political beliefs during the last twenty years.

Point 5:

Large Jewish enterprises, such as the baths,[36] large estates, factories, and large commercial firms are to be nationalized.

Point 6:

Prohibition of Jewish ritual slaughter of animals as being opposed to Slovak national feeling.[37]

Point 7:

Immediate closing of all Slovak synagogues in which hatred against Christians and destruction of Christians is preached.

Point 8:

Jewish doctors to be dismissed by all public hospitals and bathing establishments. Jews to dismiss at once their Christian female domestic help.

Point 9:

Immediate institution of racial restrictions in public and private law.[38]

Point 10:

Facilitation of Jewish emigration providing that a certain part of their property be left behind.

Sources: Slovenska Revolucia, pp. 47-49. *Tu rissky,* pp. 36,37.

It is Point 4 of the above anti-Jewish legislation that deserves special attention. Having stated in the broadcast of January 5 that Jewish property of right belonged to the Slovak people, the propagandist now points to the use of such property to reward the politically faithful.

Of equal interest is the end of the fourth paragraph with its ambiguous but prominent threat that "political developments in Central Europe have not yet ended." It may be that this was meant as an early warning against putting any faith in the Prague government and its democratic traditions in the light of German threats to Prague's future.

Slovak broadcast of January 13, 1939. (Excerpt)

For twenty years Slovaks fought for their political rights. They suffered, starved, and more than 300,000 of them had to leave their country to make a meager living abroad, working hard and sacrificing their health. On October 6 the light of Slovak freedom appeared on the horizon, and the Slovak people expected that at last their thousand-year-old wish would be fulfilled and Slovak bread would at last belong to Slovak natives. A few months have passed. We are approaching the opening of the Slovak diet. The following item illustrates the current situation. The *Voelkischer Beobachter* of January 13 writes as follows.[39]

"Sano Mach, the chief of the Slovak Propaganda Office, had a meeting with the secretary of the American Legation in Prague in order to discuss the emigration of Slovaks to the United States."

This item is full of significance. We are painfully touched by it and yet not ready to believe it. Only a short time ago the government declared that it would start a program for calling home Slovaks living abroad. And what really happens? We are looking for work opportunities abroad for our own Slovaks.

This is not the way to do it, honest Slovak workers are saying. It is not we who shall leave Slovakia but the Jews and those who have exploited us for twenty years. If Slovakia is unable to nourish her own sons, then those who were hostile to us for twenty years must be unconditionally made to leave.

Source: Handakten Seyss-Inquart. The document from which the broadcast has been culled contains only the above excerpt.

It would be highly surprising if the broadcast was meant as a personal attack on Mach. It appears more likely that its main point was to use Mach's meeting with Kennan to strike at what in German eyes were basic mistakes of the Slovak government in using too gradual an approach to solving the problem of unemployment. For background of the broadcast see Chapter III.

Slovak broadcast of January 15, 1939.
How the Slovak Revolution began.

On Wednesday, January 18, 1939, our thousand-year-old dream will be fulfilled. The Slovak parliament will convene its first meeting. It will approve our revolutionary resolutions and promulgate laws regulating our new Slovak life.

The history of our Slovak revolution has been a thorny one filled with blood, suffering, prison, persecution, misery, and hunger.

As is the case with all revolutions there have been some events in ours that are not yet sufficiently well known to the Slovak public. Now that parliament will endorse all our revolutionary decisions, it is fitting that we recall these events in the interest of historical truth.

One such event is the contribution of Vienna Slovaks to the Slovak revolution. Every Slovak man and woman will remember for all time that when the Central European earthquake started in September[40] it was Radio Vienna that first entered the struggle for self-determination for Slovakia through use of the spoken word. Day by day, week by week, we fought on the airwaves for the sacred rights of the Slovak people. Here are some fragments of our September broadcasts. (Here follow fragments of the broadcasts of September 21, 22, and 25, which were quoted in the chapter on pre-Munich broadcasts and will not be repeated here.)

The European crisis reached its climax on September 28, 1938. At that time,[41] the Vienna Slovaks had a memorable meeting under the chairmanship of the upstanding fighter Rudolf Vavra. Also present was (Franz) Karmasin, now state secretary and leader of the German minority in Slovakia. The secretary, Ludovit Mutnansky, gave a report on the political situation and amidst great enthusiasm read the following manifesto:

"The Slovaks present declare unanimously: We have examined the present political situation with special reference to Central Europe, according to our best knowledge and conscience, and we have reached the conclusion that the borders of the Danubian countries as drawn at the Versailles Peace Conference do not conform to the wishes of individual national groups. We are convinced that the maintenance of European balance requires that frontier adjustments be made to correspond to the just claims of individual nations and national groups. The assembled group declares that every nation has a right to its free and independent life and has the sole right for deciding its own fate.

"The Slovak people, too, request that right in view of their 1100-year-old history.

"The Czechoslovak state, founded on the basis of the various Paris peace treaties, denied to Slovaks the right to their own state. In their effort to create the so-called Czechoslovak people, they failed to recognize the existence of a separate Slovak people. We further emphasize unanimously the racial difference between the Czech and the Slovak peoples and the fact that the Slovak people share a Christian ideology while a majority of the Czech people has joined forces with that enemy of mankind Judaeo-Bolshevism. It is obvious that a further connection with the Czech people have shown clearly that they have no intention of fulfilling the Cleveland and Pittsburgh agreements.[42] During that period the Slovak people did not remotely enjoy the ethnic, cultural, economic, or social rights and conditions to which they were entitled.

By flouting agreements, which it had solemnly joined, the Czechoslovak state lost its existence and in its preent form constitutes a threat to world peace.

"We condemn vehemently the anti-national course of action of the Prague government in the Sudeten area, the use of firearms against innocent people coupled with destruction of their property. We declare our solidarity with the other national groups of the country; we understand their demand for the right of self-determination and join them in that demand.

"We ask that every national group in Czechoslovakia be given the opportunity to hold a plebiscite to decide its future and whether it wishes to become associated with another state. We gratefully recall Chancellor Adolf Hitler's speech of September 26, 1938, in which he acquainted the whole world with our peoples under the Tatra. He noted that we wished to have peace and that we want to live peacefully among the other nations of Europe as a free people in a free and independent Slovak state. We are convinced that the noble German people to which we are linked by a past of more than 1100 years will help us in our honest struggle.

"We warn our brothers in Czechoslovakia not to allow themselves to be bought by promises or by radio speeches resorting to low humor. It is a fact that the Freemason Benes is trying by recourse to force and to false statements to cheat the faithful Slovak people of their national rights and of their liberation which is so close. We address our manifesto to all Slovaks of good will. We give notice that we have founded an independent Slovak Legion, a free Slovakia, and we are determined to fight for Slovak freedom.

"We hereby call on all Slovaks under the Tatra Mountains and throughout the world to join our liberation movement and to join our legion.

"Long live the Slovak nation! Long live free Slovakia!"

A large number of telegrams of greeting were sent to the Fuehrer and Chancellor Adolf Hitler asking his help for the Slovak political struggle.

The manifesto has been distributed throughout the world by news services such as Deutsches Nachrichtenbuero, Polska Tlacova Kancelaria, and United Press, and we have thus succeeded in acquainting the world with the Slovak problem and the Slovak revolution.

At the same time the organization of the Slovak Legion began. All honest Slovaks in Vienna led by Vavra, Janotek, Klempa, Kozel, Hesek, Dvorsky, Konstantin Polak, Stefan Szomolanyi, Sedivy, Jankovic, etc. joined. Ludovit Mutnansky was made its commander and Rudolf Vavra its political adviser.

The Slovak people will never forget the courageous and manly actions of the Vienna Slovaks and their revolutionary activity.

From the bottom of our hearts we wish that the activity of the Slovak parliament may be a fruitful one and that the new Slovak laws may assure the Slovak people a better future.

Source: Tu rissky, pp. 38-41.

If the above broadcast illustrates one thing clearly it is the shaky ground, numerically speaking, on which the "Vienna Slovaks" based their claim to speak for all Slovaks. The manifesto mentioned by Mutnansky ventured to speak only for those present at the meeting, and it can be assumed that they were but a fraction of the small Vienna Slovak colony. The numbers who then joined the Slovak Legion would appear not to have been much bigger than the total of the eleven men named in the broadcast.

It is worth mentioning that the meeting addressed a telegram to Adolf Hitler the text of which is omitted from the above description. This omission occurred possibly because the content of the telegram was such to make it obvious that it spoke not for the Slovak people, nor even for Slovaks favoring independence, but merely for a small group of Slovaks willing to play the German game. The most prominent statement of the telegram was "we confidently put our fate into your hands."[43] It is worth noting that the phrase of "putting Slovakia's fate into Hitler's hands" was used again by Tiso in thanking Hitler for his meeting with Ribbentrop on October 19, 1938.[44] It was used again by Tuka who also entrusted the fate of his people to Hitler's care during his meeting with the Fuehrer in February 1939.[45]

Slovak broadcast of January 18, 1939.
The Slovak.

He has been thrown to the ground a thousand times, tortured a thousand times, had his feet weighted down with stones a thousand times. A thousand times have they cunningly stopped him in his tracks, betrayed him, forced him off his path, thrown mountains on him, drunk his blood, taken his soul, climbed on his back, vaunted themselves with his past and his language, bound him in slavery, made a beggar of him, ruined him, estranged his children from him, driven out his fathers, taken away his language, stolen his nation's property. All this has been done a thousand times, and every time the Slovak comes back to life victoriously and stands firmer, harder, more solidly and more determined than ever.

I read these lines recently and they come to mind now thinking of today's opening of the Slovak parliament in nearby old and famed Bratislava.

A thousand-year-old fervid longing of all Slovaks was fulfilled today.

We thank the Almighty for His goodness, but at the same time our thoughts wander to Ruzomberok where our great leader Andrej Hlinka rests. Without his honest struggle we would not have reached this point. We also lovingly remember the writer Martin Razus.[46] Our thanks go out to the martyrs of Cernova, Namestov, Kosice, Trnava, etc.[47] From the Slovak blood that was spilled grew our Slovak freedom and independence. It would be ungrateful not to think today of our living martyr Professor Vojtech Tuka who supplied the scientific basis for Hlinka's struggle. We think again today of how freedom grows out of blood and prison.

Today the Slovak parliament was solemnly opened in the spirit of Andrej Hlinka.

Today in this beautiful and solemn moment let us not forget the great leader Adolf Hitler who broke the chains of national groups in Central Europe and whose strong will called forth the sacred right of self-determination.Today's Slovak celebration is one of the results of his arduous task, and we must understand that without his intervention we would not have lived to see the opening of a Slovak parliament.

Our gratitude can best be shown by building strong friendship between Slovakia and Germany and by giving the German minority in Slovakia full rights. Slovak nationalism and German National Socialism will be allied in the future against the enemy of mankind.

As of today we have a Slovak parliament which will regulate Slovak life with new laws, and we have the Hlinka Guards who will see to it that those laws are obeyed. We still have a heavy task ahead of us.

It is a natural and burning desire of every nation to have an independent state. The Slovak people, too, are longing for it and are building it.

As of today the eyes of all Slovaks will be upon the Slovak parliament and upon its actions.

From the bottom of our hearts we wish that the Slovak parliament may fulfill the high hopes which the Slovak people have for it, that it may build the Slovak state and fulfill the great dream of our immortal leader Andrej Hlinka.

Sources: Slovenska Revolucia, pp. 57, 58. The version printed in *Slovenska Revolucia* does not include the last four paragraphs of the above text, but ends as follows: "The Slovak people will not stop on the road toward an independent Slovak state. Anyone who wishes this will be swept away by its iron will." *Tu rissky,* pp. 42, 43.

The very emphasis which the broadcast puts on Hitler's contribution to Slovak independence serves to weaken the glorification of Slovak strength, love of freedom, etc. which abounds in the broadcasts. It also justifies the charge of treason leveled by the Czechoslovak authorities against Slovak separatists who allied themselves with Germany for the destruction of Czechoslovakia.

Slovak broadcast of February 4, 1939.
Why are Jews doctors and pharmacists?

In 1489 the French king issued a severe decree against the Jews—he ordered that every Jew convert to Christianity. Those who refused to do so were forced to leave France. The Polish Jews turned to their chief rabbi for help and advice.

The chief rabbi sent the French Jews a message which is called the Toledo Message. It was published later in 1583 in the book *La Silva Curiosa.* One sentence of the message reads as follows: "You complain that they are threatening your lives. Let your children be baptized. Let them become doctors and apothecaries. Thus they can threaten the lives of your enemies without fear of being punished."

This advice agrees completely with the law of the Jewish cathechism, the Talmud, which says: You shall kill even the most honest of the heathen. Do not show pity to the heathen. If you see them dying or near death as a result of this, you may not save them. Of those who spill the blood of the godless (which means of Christians), the Rabbis say: "They are offering a sacrifice to God."

Jews have been following these principles and Talmudic law from the very beginning. Jews do not become doctors in order to heal patients, but in order to prepare poisons to kill gentiles. They do not become doctors to help the sick, but to take the health and life of non-Jews. Jews hate Christians.

Jewish doctors never took an interest in the healing of non-Jews or in the health of the Slovak people. They have but one aim and that is to ruin and enslave the Slovak people. It is for this very reason that it is primarily Jewish doctors who specialize in abortions and in birth control. Jewish doctors show great delight and Talmudic passion in performing abortions. They love to ruin Slovak women's bodies and minds and to cut down the growth of the Slovak people.

But the Jews themselves are told (by their religion): "Multiply like the sand of the sea!" It is remarkable that Jews did everything to propagate abortions but refused to sanction them in their own lives. Jewish doctors never performed forbidden operations on Jewish women but enjoyed immensely doing so on Christian women. We see then that Jews propagate and carry out abortions in the case of non-Jews while they themselves are to multiply like the sand of the sea.

The Slovak public expects that the Slovak parliament will decree severe penalties for doctors and others who have practiced abortions.

It is a logical demand that Slovak health be put under the sole care of Christian Slovak doctors. Slovak workers have been demanding for a long time that their care be entrusted only to Christian doctors. Particularly in the hospitals is there a preponderant number of Jewish doctors. Slovak workers and employees suffer unspeakably from them.

We cannot have any confidence in Jewish doctors. Until they are on their way to their final destination in the Holy Land let them continue practicing, but only on their fellow Jews and not on Christians.

Our fight against the Jews does not allow compromise or consideration. Let no one hide behind false Christian love. Who is surprised that in the course of the last twenty years more than 300,000 Slovaks emigrated to work in Belgian, French, and American mines, while Jews and non-Slovaks pocketed their belongings and grew rich.

The Slovak people will have their day of reckoning with the Jews at all costs.

There will be no order or well being in Slovakia as long as there is a single Jew left under the Tatra Mountains.

Sources: Slovenska Revolucia, pp. 52-54. *Tu rissky,* pp. 44, 45.

If his sentiments are assumed to be sincere, it is obvious that Mutnansky suffered from something akin to persecution mania on the Jewish question. The known facts of Mutnansky's life tend to bear this out.

Slovak broadcast of February 28, 1939.
Of Panslavic solidarity.

We must view political life and its results with cold intellect and realism.

There are many Slovak politicians who view political life as conforming to their imagination and desires. That is quite wrong.

One of the myths involved here is that of Panslavic solidarity. In recent times much has been made of it, and it is those who were never sincere in their feelings about the Slovak heart who appeal most loudly to the Slovak heart on its behalf.

We shall be quite open and ask the decisive question: Which of the Slavic peoples has been working honestly for Panslavic solidarity? The World War, and especially the last twenty years, should open our eyes. The mighty Russian nation suppressed Poles and Ukrainians mercilessly and did not grant them a life of their own. The Czech people united with the Slovaks in a joint state and tried to subjugate the Slovak people. They ended up by denying that a Slovak people even exists and no longer based their argument (for union) on economic grounds.

The Poles deny their Ukrainian minority an independent national life, and the same is done by the Serbs to the Croats.

It was the Poles who took a merciless bite out of young Slovakia at the time we gained our independence and who cruelly detached a part of our land that had never been Polish.[48] Is this an example of Slavic fraternalism or of Panslavic solidarity?

Every Slavic nation conducts its past and present foreign policy according to its own needs. This can be seen from claims made by all Slavic nations without regard to others, even to other Slavic states. For we Slovaks this is a good lesson for the future.

Now that the Slovak people have arisen and are on their way to independent statehood, clever political gangsters operating uncer cover of a nonexistent Panslavic solidarity are trying to pull the Slovak people back under their exploitation and suppression. No, never again.

The Slovak people will not stop on the road toward an independent Slovak state. Anyone who wishes this will be swept away by its iron will. We go by the motto of the Rodobrana: "To have one's own independent state means life, liberty, eternity; not to have a Slovak state means death, eternal death for the Slovak people."

And the Slovak people wish to have a long and beautiful life. Therefore brothers and sisters, let us go forward with an iron will to build our eternal life —the independent Slovak state.

Sources: Slovenska Revolucia, pp. 65, 66. *Tu rissky,* pp. 46, 47.

The topic treated in this broadcast portends of things to come. After World War II had begun and as German victory became less and less certain, many Slovaks felt pangs of conscience for having betrayed their Czech brothers, while others looked toward their Slavic neighbors in Russia for help in ousting the Germans. Both sentiments were prevalent in the blood-soaked Slovak rebellion against the Germans in 1944.

Slovak broadcast of March 2, 1939.
From Orava: Impressive demonstrations for the Slovak state in Orava and Liptova.

It all started in Risnovce.[49] A crowd of tens of thousands enthusiastically expressed its agreement with a nationalistic speech of Sano Mach[50] who spoke as follows: "The ideals for which we suffered for twenty years, for which we were jailed and ruined, have become our program. We want and we will get our independent Slovak state."

The first official declaration of the Slovak government was equally a declaration in favor of Slovak independence.[5H]

On Saturday there was a Slovak propaganda meeting in Ruzomberok and on Sunday in Liptovsky St. Mikulas. The speech of Sano Mach left a powerful impression, and the Slovak people made a unanimous and enthusiastic demonstration for Slovak independence, for the Slovak government, and for the Slovak martyr Professor Vojtech Tuka.

All Slovakia has formed a united front for independence and for free development of the physical and mental resources of the Slovak soil and people.
From Belgium: Slovaks abroad see the security of the Slovak future only in an independent state. . .

Source: Slovenska Revolucia, p.75.

The above broadcast was followed on March 3 by one in which a letter from Slovak students at Prague University belonging to the Hlinka Party was read. The letter expressed support for Tuka and Mach in their demand for complete Slovak independence.

Slovak broadcast of March 4, 1939.
We just received the following news report from Bratislava.

The police in Bratislava have been put on the alert. Radio cars and patrols have been doubled. Reinforcements are coming in from Bohemia and Moravia. All over Slovakia police and gendarmes have been put on the alert because of well-founded fears of anti-Jewish and anti-Czech demonstrations. Slovak workers have gone on strike and do not want to remain under Jewish and Czech rule any longer. The situation in Slovakia is becoming tense. *Source: Slovenskia Revolucia,* p. 75. This broadcast shows that the situation in Slovakia undoubtedly has taken a turn for the worse, and it also shows that radio Vienna is doing all in its power to emphasize reports of unrest and to fan this unrest.

Slovak broadcast of March 5, 1939.

The chairman of the Slovak government, Dr. Jozef Tiso, was asked by the Prague government to state openly and frankly whether or not Slovakia wished to remain part of the Czechoslovak Republic. The chairman replied that if Slovaks were satisfied they would remain; if they were not, they would separate. This question had been adequately answered by the first official declaration of the Slovak government. The chairman of the Slovak government had not once mentioned the Czechoslovak state in that declaration but had spoken only of the Slovak state. Since the declaration had been approved beforehand by all members of the cabinet, it would appear that all Slovak ministers have made the political concept of an independent Slovak state their own.

We have already reported how Orava and Liptava reacted enthusiastically to the idea of an independent Slovak state, and we have also informed our listeners how Slovaks abroad and Hlinka Party students in Prague are urging the creation of an independent state.[52]

(We cite) the prophetic words spoken by Professor Tuka to the Slovak nation when all Slovakia welcomed him in triumph on December 9, 1938. (Here follows Tuka's speech as reported in the broadcast of December 9. It will not be repeated here.)

Always keep in mind the struggle and suffering that our great leader Andrej Hlinka endured. His actions were not intended to benefit a few hundred people, but to free the Slovak people and to improve their condition. Slovak men and women! The great struggle of Andrej Hlinka is not yet over. It will be ended only when the Slovak people live in their own independent state. On to battle, Slovaks! Our battle will be over only when we have an independent state. Only then will we be able to sing with a clear conscience: Andrej Hlinka is resting in peace—Slovakia is suffering no more.

It should be noted that the Slovaks in the Greater German Reich published a manifesto during their great Vienna meeting of September 29, 1938, when the world crisis was at its peak, from which we cite the following historic passage: "We wish to have peace and to live peacefully among the other nations of Europe as a free people in a free and independent Slovak state."[53]

The development of Slovak political events after October 6 shows clearly that we can safeguard our future only in an independent Slovak state.

Slovak writes as follows: "The Prague parliament will definitely have to settle down to its first spring session. Appearances must be kept up, but what about content? What will this rump parliament in Prague discuss? It will not contain a single Ruthenian deputy. They all lost their seats due to the plans of the Volosin government.[57] There are no Germans there either other than two or three who are only interested in listening to deputy Kundt.[55] Kundt, a former deputy of the Henlein Party[56] is a likeable man. He makes the rounds of the ministries and government offices demanding more rights for the Germans of Bohemia and Moravia. He resists being sidetracked. He always refers to the deputy of the Slovakian Germans Karmasin and points out what the Slovak government has achieved for its Germans on his recommendations.

Rumors are flying and fortune-tellers are lately in great demand in Prague. They are visited also by important gentlemen who let them read their future in the cards and occasionally also that of the nation.

Who knows what will come? What will the situation be like a week or a month from today?

Source: Slovenska Revolucia, pp. 76-78.

The above broadcast is a brief anthology of major pronouncements in favor of Slovak separatism and ends by quoting an article of the Hlinka Party newspaper stressing the atmosphere of tension and foreboding then prevailing, the point of the quotation obviously being to use that atmosphere to further promote Slovak separatism.

<u>Slovak broadcast of March 6, 1939.</u>

Every day we receive many letters from Slovakia and from our brothers in Bohemia, Hungary, Poland, France, Belgium, and elsewhere. This fact demonstrates clearly that the Slovak broadcasts from Vienna are an absolute necessity. Every day we receive thanks for our news service and for our struggle to complete Hlinka's battle. There are also those who do not understand the purpose of our news reports. This gives us a welcome opportunity to discuss the question why the Slovak minority in Greater Germany has been broadcasting a program of news and what this indicates.

The gigantic unification process and the equally gigantic activity of National Socialism in Greater Germany has had an intellectual influence on the Slovaks who live here. The Slovaks in Greater Germany have had the opportunity to study the difference between the so-called democratic system and the constructive activity of National Socialism, and they insist that a similar constructive effort take place in our Slovak home under the Tatra Mountains. That is why we point out daily harmful and hostile Slovak developments and why we mercilessly expose cancers in the Slovak body public. We point out the anti-national exploitation practiced by Jews and other strangers. Slovaks know who our worst enemies are, they are the Jews and their mercenaries. In a manner approaching genius they take over Slovak economic affairs with the help of the Freemasons. Prague has recognized that weakness long ago and that is why it used the Jews to destroy the Slovaks and to maintain its own power.

We see the unique efforts made by the responsible Slovak governmental authorities to solve that question, but there are certain circumstances why the struggle against the enemies of the Slovak people cannot be fought as vigorously on Radio Bratislava as it can on Radio Vienna.

Unfortunately the power of Prague and of Freemasonry can still be felt in Slovakia, and it is that power which does not wish Radio Bratislava to fight an uncompromising battle.

For this very reason we feel that Radio Vienna is performing a valuable service and that it spurs action on many important issues. Undoubtedly it also serves the leading Slovak political figures and the government who are still struggling against hard and determined opponents.

The issue of overriding importance today is to fight Andrej Hlinka's great battle to the finish and thus to build a free Slovakia. To accomplish this objective Slovaks all over the world must contribute according to their ability.

It is clear that the Slovak minority in Greater Germany, using Radio Vienna as its medium, is following the path of our immortal leader Andrej Hlinka in its struggle to build an independent Slovak state and to uplift the Slovak people.

Source: Slovenska Revolucia, pp. 78, 79.

It is not without significance that the opposition to the Vienna broadcasts was apparently of such importance and strength that a considerable part of the above broadcast was used to defend the idea of the broadcasts and their motivation. The role of Radio Vienna in prodding the Slovak government to take those measures the broadcasts considered important is here expressed with great frankness.

Slovak broadcast of March 9, 1939.
Let us build up our Hlinka Guard in the East.

The fact that in less than a month's time thousands upon thousands of Slovaks have joined the Hlinka Guards without agitation or sizeable organizational effort shows the sound instinct and verve of the Slovak people which have always kept us going even when our intellectuals dropped by the way or when times were at their worst. The Guards grew with sudden vehemence and enthusiastically set themselves in motion from west to east. All Slovakia became enthralled by the Guards, and our revolution somehow took place under the protecting shadow of the Guards who were the terror of the parasites of the Slovak people and who kept up our courage in the worst of times.

To be a member of the Hlinka Guards must be an honor, a duty, a national duty for everyone. Let us not be overoptimistic about our situation. We have so many problems that our entire people must be constantly alert. Every able-bodied young man must be a Guardist, a soldier of the Slovak people. We must continue to build and to improve the organization of our Hlinka Guards. Let us pay increased attention to Eastern Slovakia. Our Eastern Slovak young men have always been steadfast autonomists. Today, they, too, understand where their duty as Slovaks lies and that is why the organizers of the Hlinka Guard must now concentrate with special interest on the East. They must build and strengthen the Eastern Guard of Hlinka Slovakia. The Hlinka Guard has a hard and important task ahead of it. Behind it stands steadfastly the Slovak government and the entire Slovak people from the Carpatho-Ukraine to the Czech border, from our famed Tatra Mountains to the Danube.

Not only the Slovaks beneath the Tatra Mountains but those abroad as well stand united behind our Slovak army and our Hlinka Guards. Today's watchword must be: One people, one Guard, one Slovak state.

Source: Slovenska Revolucia, p. 80.

This broadcast, like the preceding one, allows us to recognize certain weaknesses. It indicates that recruitment for the Hlinka Guards was lagging, especially in Eastern Slovakia; it further shows that many of those joining the Guard did so as late as February 1939, which would indicate that they did not join from enthusiasm but for opportunistic reasons. The point mentioned in the broadcast that the Slovak revolution took place under the protecting shadow of the Hlinka Guards also cannot be viewed as an indication of popular enthusiasm. Finally, the stress on recruitment in Eastern Slovakia may be seen as an indication that the propagandists knew that drastic changes were about to take place and that the protection of the Slovak border furthest away from Germany was of particular importance.

[1]In the case of Carpatho-Ukrainian autonomy the Prague government had already granted some preliminary concessions in the summer of 1937.

[2]*Slovak* was the party organ of the Slovak People's Party.

[3]Rodobrana, a Slovak Fascist paramilitary organization, was founded by Tuka in 1923.

[4]In 1937.

[5]The reference is to Ferdinand Durcansky, minister of justice under the new autonomous Slovak government, formed on October 7, 1938.

[6]Reference to Hitler's remark in his speech at Sportpalast on September 26, 1938, that he did not want any Czechs.

[7]Reference to the visit of Slovakia's new Premier Tiso to Germany's Foreign Minister Ribbentrop on October 19, 1938.

[8]This introductory paragraph preceded all Slovak language broadcasts at the time and will not be repeated for each broadcast. Its slogan was a favorite of the People's Party. See also Chapter I, footnote 16.

[9]For a reference to Derer's role in the Tuka trial see broadcast of October 24, 1938. It explains the special hostility shown to him by the propagandists.

[10]The Social Democratic Party was banned in Slovakia in October 1938, and Prime Minister Tiso announced during that same month that henceforth there would be only an official National Union Party.

[11]The so-called Vienna Award of November 2, 1938 had turned over considerable areas of Slovakia as well as of the Carpatho-Ukraine to Hungary.

[12]The Zips region in northeastern Slovakia adjoining Poland was an old German-speaking enclave.

[13]Franz Karmasin was the spokesman for the German minority in the Slovak government.

[14]Eduard Benes had resigned the presidency of Czechoslovakia on October 5, 1938, following the Munich Agreement.

[15]Thomas G. Masaryk was the founder and first president of Czechoslovakia.

[16]No such list formed part of the text of this broadcast. A later broadcast, that of December 22, 1938, contains a list of Freemasons.

[17]Tuka was accused of working for Hungarian interests.

[18]Dr. Tuka returned to Bratislava on December 6, 1938.

[19]Reference to Jaroslav Hasek's *The Good Soldier Schweik,* whose behavior has become a classic example of passive resistance.

[20]Date of the Munich Agreement.

[21]*Voelkischer Beobachter,* Vienna edition, November 30, 1938, p. 2.

[22]*Voelkischer Beobachter,* Vienna edition, November 10, 1938, p. 6.

[23]This is literally a double cross. The Slovak cross consists of two horizontal bars.

[24]Tiso's decision to take a surprise nationality census on December 31, 1938 was probably influenced by lessons of the Munich Agreement. The agreement

had failed to define what percentage of German minority population would constitute the basis for cession. As a result Germany could and did interpret the percentage in her own favor thus adding to Czech uncertainty and to Czech territorial losses. Tiso apparently wanted to nip in the bud future pressures on the part of the Slovak German minority. The attempt backfired. however, and Tiso subsequently had to give in to a number of German minority demands.

[25]This is the date of the Zilina Agreement of the major Slovak parties in favor of demanding autonomy from the Prague government.

[26]Typical Jewish names.

[27]Deutsche Partei, successor to the Karpatendeutsche Partei, was the political spokesman of the German minority in Slovakia.

[28]Reference to the Zilina Agreement.

[29]Jozef Srobar was the brother of Dr. Vavro Srobar, one of the leading Slovak followers of President Masaryk. His praise for Sidor was therefore of special significance.

[30]Reference to the Zilina Agreement.

[31]An ironic reference to the Biblical statement, "the laborer is worthy of his hire" (Luke: 10.7) and to the passive attitude of some of the clerical-minded toward labor demands.

[32]End of sentence missing.

[33]The reasons for his fall from favor with the German propagandists were his pro-Polish stance and the fact that he had sided with Slovak moderates in the discussions with President Hacha during the latter's visit to Slovakia in late 1938.

[34]Reference to a border incident between Czechoslovak and Hungarian troops near Munkacs (Mukacevo) on January 6, 1939.

[35]Reference to the parts of Slovakia ceded to Hungary by the Vienna Award of November 2, 1938.

[36]The large Slovak spa of Piestany was allegedly Jewish owned or managed. See also biographical sketch of Ludovit Mutnansky for his personal connections with Piestany.

[37]The accusation that Jewish ritual slaughtering is inhumane has been held against the Jews in many areas and periods. The answer of the Jews, often supported by expert opinion, is usually that the method of cutting the animal's throat to drain its blood before killing it will, if properly handled, render the animal unconscious and thus make its subsequent death virtually painless.

[38]What is referred to here is the institution in Slovakia of the "Arier-paragraph" of the German Nuremberg Laws of 1935, or its equivalent.

[39]*Voelkischer Beobachter,* Vienna edition, January 13, 1939, p. 5.

[40]Reference to the Munich crisis of September 1938.

[41]The date of the meeting was September 29, 1938. See *Voelkischer Beobachter,* Vienna edition, September 30, 1938, p. 8; also, Petreas, *Die Slowakei im Umbruch,* p. 69.

[41]The Cleveland agreement between Czechs and Slovaks in the United States for a postwar federal state was signed October 22, 1915.

[43]*Voelkischer Beobachter,* Vienna edition, September 30, 1938, p. 8.

[44]See *ADAP* IV, p. 89.

[45]See *IMT,* 2790-PS.

[46]Razus was one of the leading Slovak autonomists. He died in 1937.

[47]Cernova was the site of a famous Hungarian-Slovak crash in 1907, leading to the death of fifteen Slovak men and women. Namestov, Kosice and Trnava were sites of clashes resulting from People's Party demonstrations in the 1920's.

[48]Reference to the cession by Slovakia to Poland of about 167 square kilometers with 8,000 inhabitants following an agreement reached on November 1, 1938.

[49]Sano Mach's speech of February 5, 1939 at Risnovce may be seen as the start of a greater degree of Slovak involvement for independence.While it is true that Tuka had demanded full independence in a public speech on December 9, 1938 at Bratislava, it was now the first time that an official of the Slovak government did so. For other sources of information on Mach's speech see Petreas, *Die Slowakei im Umbruch,* p. 131, and *Voelkischer Beobachter,* Vienna edition, February 6, 1939, p. 2.

[5]Sano Mach had become propaganda chief of the Slovak government on October 16, 1938. He remained one of its most prominent officials throughout World War II.

[51]Reference to the governmental declaration of February 21, 1939, stressing Slovak independence and ignoring the Czechoslovak state.

[52]See broadcasts of March 2 and 3, 1939.

[53]See broadcast of January 15, 1939.

[54]Mgr. Augustin Volosin was premier of autonomous Ruthenia, Slovakia's eastern neighbor province, between October 1938 and March 1939.

[55]Ernst Kundt was the spokesman for Germans in the Czech part of Czechoslovakia following the Munich Agreement and prior to March 1939.

[56]Sudeten German Party, the National Socialist oriented party of Germans in Czechoslovakia, led by Konrad Henlein.

CHAPTER VIII

RADIO WAR[1]

After March 9, 1939 events rapidly came to a head. Internally, the dismissal of the Tiso Government by President Hacha on March 10 created excitement and nervousness. Externally, the crescendo of German propaganda from Vienna to which Dr. Durcansky and others lent their names and authority added fuel to the flames of domestic disunity. Heavy political and military pressure by the German Government against the governments in Prague and Bratislava aimed to force the former into submission and the latter into declaring its independence from Prague. Pressure and propaganda supplemented each other in achieving another bloodless victory for the Germans in both their endeavors thus completing, in effect, their earlier bloodless victory at Munich.

Durcansky broadcast of March 10, 1939, 2100 hours.
Men and women of Slovakia!

Few of us expected to reach the point at which we find ourselves today as quickly as we did. It has not been so very long since the deluded policies of the Czech leaders brought not only their own nation, but our Slovak people as well, to the very edge of catastrophe. Every on e of us believed that the Czech people would by now have learned their lesson and would avoid any action that might threaten the existence of the republic and national survival itself. But we were wrong. The Czech people and their leaders have learned nothing from history or from their own past mistakes. On the contrary, they have concentrated their efforts on depriving we Slovaks of the rights that we acquired after twenty years of suffering. Since October they have been searching for every pretext for doing so. It would have been impossible for them to accomplish anything in this direction, however, had it not been for dubious and traitorous elements in our own people such as Teplansky[2] who have been eagerly waiting to regain the power they formerly held. Prague has indeed found men in our midst who are more interested in gaining her favor than in the rights and freedom of their own people.

Since October the Slovak government has made a great mistake—it has not taken the energetic, purposeful, and drastic action required against these destructive and dangerous elements. What has so far been neglected, however, must be corrected tomorrow or, at any rate, within the next few days. The dubious elements that turn everything to their own advantage and are out for their own selfish interests must disappear once and for all from the Slovak scene. The time when men who had nothing in common with the Slovak spirit or Slovak life held power in Slovakia is over and will never be allowed to return.

We, the legal representatives of the Slovak people, have now again, as so often in the past, been attacked treacherously. Prague has always worked against us, behind our backs. When the Slovak autonomy laws were about to be passed, and many times since then, attempts were made to convince us that it was impossible for us to act, or to survive, without Prague. Every step we took met with resistance. Inconspicuously, efforts were made to whittle down and to do away with our autonomy, and there were Slovak ministers who had no intention of resisting those efforts to the utmost of their ability. Prague did everything to cut down the prestige of our government in the eyes of our own people by employing such measures as having the National Bank refuse us the right to float our own loans, while the Prague government used these very loans for its own purposes. They tried thus to force us down on our knees. When the Slovak government became aware of Prague's purpose, however, when it refused to relinquish its rights but insisted on upholding the interest of its people, and when the Tiso government declared that Slovak national interest would be the sole guide of its present and future policy, Prague began to see clearly that its efforts were bound to fail. It was then decided to remove the government, or rather those in the government, who stood in Prague's way.

At first this succeeded. Prague found men who for reasons of fear or of self-interest lent themselves to fight against those ideals so sacred and dear to every Slovak heart and for which every one of us is willing to risk his life. Every nation has its weaklings and we are no exception. Men of Teplansky's ilk were found who were ready to betray their people, to make untrue public statements, and to submit to everything due to their bad conscience. The Slovak people have long since reached a verdict about them and will never again believe them. The Slovaks know them now from their own experience and will indicate this to them, such as was done at a meeting of Minister Teplansky when members of his audience turned their coats around to show him what they thought of his "political agility." They foresaw that this chameleon would not pursue policies in the people's interest.

The action of the Prague government is illegal. It is based on the facts that Prague controls the armed forces, that Czech officers command Slovak regiments, and that we were so trusting and passive as to allow Czechs and dubious Slovaks to keep key positions, men who are opposed to the idea of Slovaks being masters in their own house, to outside domination being ended, and to the idea that they must start to make a living from the work of their own hands rather than from the dubious funds received for betraying the Slovak people. The action of the Prague government is illegal because it is not based on the Constitution. According to the Constitutional Law on Slovak Autonomy, the President of the Republic appoints the Slovak government on the basis of the recommendation submitted to him by the president of the Slovak Diet. The Slovak government can be deposed only if it no longer enjoys the confidence of the Diet or if it resigns of its own free will. Neither of these two things has happened and the Slovak government thus cannot be deposed, nor is anyone authorized to appoint a new government to take its place. In deposing the previous government and appointing a new one, the president of the republic acted illegally and in violation of the solemn oath of office which he took upon his election.The Slovak people have thus again been shown that Czechs and their representatives never keep their promises.

The consequence of this illegal action on the part of Prague is that the Tiso government continues to exist and to exercise lawful authority. I myself as member of that government am aware that to do so is not fully possible in view of the fact that the Czech soldiery simply executes the orders given by Mr. Teplansky's cold dictatorship. What the generals who, apparently, are happy to have been spared the task of proving their ability in the fall[3] are now doing goes beyond all limits of law and justice. It is impossible for General Homola simply to declare martial law in Slovakia because he is eager for adventures and because this suits the desires of the gentlemen in Prague.[4] A general of this kind should be taken to court at once.

Prague must at long last realize that the time has passed when one could govern in the manner which it is again attempting when ministers are dismissed at night; when men like Mach and Tuka, who enjoy the confidence of the people, are apprehended and arrested at night; when government offices are seized by the military; when the radio is abused by the ridiculous Teplansky government, and so on. Those times are gone forever, and proof of this, among others, is the fact that I am here spaking to you. I am the legal representative of the Slovak people; I have been called into office by the will of that people, and I assure everyone of you that I will not disappoint you.

Men and women of Slovakia!

There will be dubious characters whispering that I am doing all this on my own. I declare to you, I am acting on the basis of a detailed, thoroughly considered discussion and with the approval of all those members of the government who have been appointed by your decision of December 18, 1938 and of February 23, 1939[5] and who are to be considered the rightful representatives of the Slovak people. I know that Prague will do anything to prove me wrong. I believe, however, that you cannot and will not believe them; for how could you believe fairytales spread by the Prague news agency, which was still trying to tell you this morning that everything that is taking place is being done with the approval of the responsible Slovak officials. In reality, only Teplansky agreed, while the rest of us either did not know about it or, as in the case of Sidor,[6] have opposed it and protested against it.

Stay at your posts! Do not believe the so-called official news from Prague or Bratislava. They are lies and bear no resemblance to the truth. Resist whenever necessary. Do not succumb to provocations! And most important of all, let the Hlinka Guards gradually assemble in all areas, in every city, town, and village. They are to take over power and to see to it that public order is maintained. Whoever resists this, or attempts to restrain it, is an enemy of the Slovak people.

Prague has abused the power it held, and it is now up to us to take power into our on hands. This requires Slovak unity. Slovak power must reside in Slovak hands alone. Every Slovak policeman, gendarme, or soldier must put himself at the service of Slovak law of the Slovak government, and of law and order. In doing this he should wear the armband of the Hlinka Guards to show that he is acting in accordance with the interests of the Slovak people, with Hlinka's wishes, and with the orders of his superiors. Let no one be doubtful or hesistant. Let each do his duty. At the same time, public order must be maintained, and all vital economic activity must continue in the interest of the Slovak people. Czech orders, and orders from traitors like Teplansky, are not binding on you, it now having become clear beyond a doubt that the Czechs are pursuing nothing but their own interests and that they are doing so exclusively at our expense and at that of our children. Those Hlinka Guard detachments that serve in border communities are to man the borders so that at last we shall be masters in our own house.

Every man to his post! Wait for my further instructions. Since I am the representative of your legal government, no one but myself has the authority to give such orders, no one is in a position to speak to you freely, at least for the next few days. My orders, particularly regarding the action of the Hlinka Guards, are to be scrupulously obeyed since I am an officer of that Slovak organization whose higher leaders are not now in a position to give you instructions which they consider necessary to our people's interest.

Our enemies, Czechs and traitorous Slovaks, should know that every attempt to oppose the legitimate government will be punished severely. The transition in which we find ourselves will pass, and I assure you that we shall secure the national rights of the Slovak people as envisaged by the executive committee of the Hlinka Party at its meeting in Zilina on October 6 of last year.

Stay at your posts! The Hlinka Guard should gradually take over power where it is not already in reliable Slovak hands. See to it that public order is maintained, and accept the services of all Slovak gendarmes and policemen who volunteer them. As for you, Czechs and "Czechoslovaks," however, resign voluntarily so that you do not cause even greater misery to your people.

Men and women of Slovakia! Guardists!

I call upon you to fight for our national freedom which we aim to achieve with the help of our friends, the great German nation.

Na straz.[7]

Sources: Handakten Seyss-Inquart. Kovar, "Notizen aus den Maerztagen 1939," pp. 7-10. *Slovenska Revolucia* rr. 82-86; *Tu rissky,* pp. 48-52. *Voelkischer Beobachter, Vienna edition,* March 12-13, 1939, p. 5.

The opening statement in the "radio war" between Germany and Slovak separatists on the one hand, and Prague and Slovak loyalists on the other, was made by Ferdinand Durcansky, Tiso's minister of transport, who with German help had made his way to Vienna following President Hacha's dismissal of the Tiso government. Durcansky spoke over the Vienna radio at 2100 hours on March 10, less that twenty-four hours after the Tiso government's dismissal. His speech is an open appeal for peaceful, but complete secession of Slovakia from the Czechoslovak state with the Slovak Hlinka Guards seizing control and Czech troops and Slovak loyalists in effect being asked to cease all resistance against this seizure of power. Durcansky's argument that President Hacha's action in dismissing the Tiso government was illegal is weakened in retrospect by the fact that his German friends had at first tried to pressure Karol Sidor, the man appointed by Hacha to replace Tiso, to declare himself in favor of Slovak independence. It was only after Sidor had adamantly refused to yield to this German pressure that the "illegality" of Hacha's action was given full play by the German propaganda machine. The other, and perhaps more fundamental weakness of Durcansky's argument was that he was in effect using the Constitutional Law on Autonomy granted by the Czechoslovak state as criterion of legality, while at the same time calling for the dismemberment of the state that had passed that law. The official Czech point of view explaining disZ missal of the Tiso government was, in fact, that it had proved itsel strong enough in resisting separatist pressures against the state.

There can be little doubt that Durcansky's final reference to German support for Slovak separatism will not have escaped the attention of his listeners at a time when fear of Germany was paralyzing most of Europe, and the fact that Durcansky was addressing his countrymen from a German radio station must have convinced his listeners that his assurances of German support were indeed well founded.

It is difficult to gauge accurately the impact of Durcansky's speech on Slovak public opinion. In the absence of anything resembling a popular uprising in favor of secession such as Durcansky had been urging, some authors have concluded that his speech evaporated without any effect.[8] Some proof of this contention can be seen in a dispatch to the Berlin Foreign Office by Seyss-Inquart, who reports on the day following Durcansky's speech that its effect was excellent but was largely dissipated by Karol Sidor who, addressing the Slovak nation over Radio Bratislava at 1015 hours on March 11, had appealed for calm and had very strongly urged the Hlinka Guards, of whom he was commander in chief, to maintain the strictest discipline.[9]

Taking a somewhat larger view, however, it is likely that appeals such as Durcansky's, coming from a former minister and giving ample evidence of German support for Slovak secession, were bound to have an aggregate impact on the Slovak people, especially when, as was to be the case, they were repeated during the following days. That impact, though it never reached the proportions hoped for by Durcansky, was nonetheless tangible and consisted of convincing the masses of the Slovak people that it would be most unwise to take any action in support of Czechoslovak unity. This apathy of the majority made it possible for the separatist minority to take over the leadership of the nation.[10]

Slovak broadcast from Vienna: March 11, 1939, 1200 hours.

Bratislava reports:

Based on a continuous flow of news and telephone calls the following situation report emerges for our Vienna Slovaks.

Sidor's actions are puzzling to the entire Slovak public.[11] One is reminded of the critical days of September when Sidor also made a speech. Two words were missing among the many which he used yesterday—Czechs and Jews. The independence and sovereignty of the Slovak state no longer appear in his program. When the Slovak masses asked for Teplansky's dismissal as proof of the government's representing their interests, Sidor refused. The reasons for this are not unknown even abroad. The tactics of the Prague government have not changed. The Slovak public cannot interpret these actions other than as treason. There is talk about this not being his (Sidor's) first, but his last treasonable deed. The tradition of the glorious Hlinka Guards now rests on the shoulders of its energetic chief of staff Murgas who will not disappoint the hopes of its members throughout the nation.

Source: Teletype no. 788 of March 11, 1939, 1400 hours, from Dr. Hammerschmid of Seyss-Inquart's staff to Dr. Lohse, Foreign Office, Berlin. Handakten Seyss-Inquart.

An exact comparison of the Seyss-Inquart teletype no. 785 referred to in footnote 9 with the above broadcast shows how the voice of the "Vienna Slovaks" was actually that of Seyss-Inquart and his staff. The references of the broadcast to the absence of the words Czechs and Jews and to the absence of separatist tendencies in Sidor's speech are almost identical with Seyss-Inquart's message to Berlin.

It is also significant that the above broadcast refers to "Slovak masses" demanding Teplansky's dismissal, while the Seyss-Inquart teletype referring to the same event had merely mentioned this demand being made of Sidor by Guardists who were expecting him at the railraod station upon his return from Prague on March 10.

The special significance of the broadcast lies in the fact that it shows the swift withdrawal of Seyss-Inquart's earlier support for Sidor following Sidor's rebuff to the radical separatists in his party. Seyss-Inquart thus came out quite openly against Sidor at a time when German official policy was still bent on winning Sidor's backing for Slovak independence and shifted his support to Karol Murgas, chief of staff of the Hlinka Guards.

The broadcast not only shows the extent of Seyss-Inquart's interference in Slovak affairs but also points to the fact that in this instance Seyss-Inquart was actually ahead of official Berlin policy, due no doubt to the fact that he was much closer to Bratislava and more familiar with Slovak events than most Berlin officials.

Slovak broadcast from Vienna: March 11, 1939, 1300 hours.
Disquieting news continues to arrive from Bratislava. In view of the hopelessness of the situation, grave friction has arisen within the group siding with the Czechs and Jews, and this has led to personal conflict. Minister Teplansky planned to call in Czech troops again. In addition there has been a constant attempt to give the appearance that Prime Minister Tiso supports what is taking place. In reality Tiso has vigorously refused to lend his support to a new compromise that would be worse than the one agreed upon in November.[12] Attacks against Germans are increasing. In the Kremnica area the German teacher Rott was arrested and maltreated by Czech gendarmes.

Source: Teletype no. 789 of March 11, 1939, 1416 hours, from Dr. Hammerschmid of Seyss-Inquart's staff to Dr. Lohse, Foreign Office, Berlin. Handakten Seyss-Inquart.

In addition to the attempt to depict Slovak loyalists as a small group backing Czechs and Jews, the above broadcast is also noteworthy for its refusal to recognize the preceding day's deposition of Tiso to whom it still refers as prime minister.

Durcansky broadcast of March 12, 1939, 1400 hours.
Slovaks! Guardists!
The situation in Slovakia, as you know, has reached a point where our best men, proven fighters of the People's Party and deputies of the Slovak Diet, have been arrested and interned. Others who refused to abstain from political activity in this very critical moment of Slovak history have had to go into hiding. Free political speech impossible. Every public expression of opinion is controlled by armed and uniformed Czechs. The press and radio are under supervision. Only those of our former political fellow workers are still at liberty who Prague expects will accept a solution that will be forced upon our people with bayonets. Prague is working with men who it expects will still try to find a solution within a Czech republic regardless of the dead and wounded.
The Slovak people cannot and will not accept any further compromise and lawlessness. Let there be an end to compromise and indecision. We need a solution that conforms to the will of the Slovak people. This solution will come in *the very near future.* Let everyone of you stand at his post to defend the interests of the Slovak people. Be patient and resolute. Let everyone see to it that governmental power is put into Slovak hands, that order, power, and discipline

be exercised only by upright Slovaks, so that *in the decisive hour which may come at any moment* Slovaks alone will be masters of Slovakia.

Do not fear battle or sacrifice; be resolute and patient.

Slovaks! Guardists! *The hour for which you have all been waiting will soon strike. Be ready.* Be on guard.

Sources: Alexander Henderson, Eyewitness in Czechoslovakia (London: George C. Harrap & Co., 1939), p. 309. Kovar, "Notizen aus den Maerztagen 1939," p. 19. *Schulthess' Europaeischer Geschichtskalender 1939* (Munich: C.H. Beck'sche Verlagsbuchhandlung,1940), pp. 280, 281. *Neues Wiener Tagblatt,* March 14, 1939. *The New York Times,* March 13, 1939.

Durcansky's speech of March 12 had been preceded during the night of March 11-12 by repeated announcements over Radio Vienna that an important message from Slovakia would soon be forthcoming. This message was to have been nothing less than the Slovak declaration of independence which Durcansky had prepared for German approval. Under the impact of Sidor's refusal to go along with their wishes the German government decided, however, that it was too soon to lend its support to what was essentially the declaration of one man, namely Durcansky, and its announcement on the radio had to be postponed. Durcansky's speech was bound to appear anticlimactic, and it is almost certainly due to this circumstance that its most prominent characteristics are the repeated promises of speedy action. Interestingly enough, these promises (italicized above) were all eliminated from the text carried by the German press. They could too easily have been interpreted abroad as threats of German intervention in Slovak affairs as indeed Durcansky must have meant them to be interpreted by his Slovak listeners.[13]

Speech of Karol Murgas, March 13, 1939, 1200 hours.[14]

The cowardly mercenaries of Prague have spread the news that I went abroad as early as Thursday, March 9. In reality it was not until this morning that I gave the necessary orders to the true leaders and messengers of my staff in the Hlinka Guards and then crossed through a cordon of Czech gendarmes and police, who have been given Hlinka Guard armbands by our present masters, to come here. It is not my fault that I had to cross the border at the risk of my life and that I had to ask our Vienna friends to make it possible for me to address you Hlinka Guardists, my old comrades in arms, over the radio. Last night I tried to speak on Radio Bratislava but found that the Czech gendarmes permit our Hlinka Guards in the building of the radio station only if Sidor, Sokol, Stano, or Zatko[15] and the others now in power wish to speak. If, however, Tiso, Durcansky, Mach, Tuka, or Murgas tried to speak there, the Bratislava radio station would be occupied at once by Czech terrorists wearing false armbands. That is the truth—everything else is a lie.

Guardists! Comrades in arms! At six o'clock on the morning of March 10, twenty minutes before it was occupied by Czech terrorists, I left the staff office of the Hlinka Guards; but I remained in Bratislava and gave orders to my comrades from my home. I obtained arms and planned for the defense of the Bratislava area. I have kept the oath that I took in memory of our immortal leader Andrej Hlinka and his last will for Slovakia. For that reason my command post was seized last night by men acting in the so-called "Sidor spirit." Spies and paid informers have tried to uncover everyone of my steps and intentions. Yesterday afternoon Karol Sidor announced on the radio that over 200 Hlinka Guard leaders who have been taken to Moravia as hostages will be freed this morning. This means that Tuka, Mach, Cernak, and all the others should have been in Bratislava or their other home towns—Trencin, Zilina, Banska-Bystrica, Ruzomberok. The present prime minister Sidor said verbatim: "We have at once lifted all military measures and have returned governmental authority to civilian hands." We found, however, that as of yesterday evening there were cordons manned by soldiers on all street corners of Bratislava. According to Sidor's words the gates of all army barracks in the Bratislava area should have been opened this morning. Let the present prime minister open those gates to show the people there are no tanks manned by Czech terrorists in the barracks yards and that soldiers of Slovak nationality are not being interned and treated like prisoners. Let Slovak troops commanded by Slovak officers at last be seen in the streets of Bratislava, Trencin, Piestany, Ruzomberok, Bystrica. Only when Slovak regiments, divisions, and army corps are under Slovak command will one be able to speak of a truly *Slovak* government and of Slovak independence. I have separated from Prime Minister Sidor in an open and honest way. I spoke to him at five o'clock on the afternoon of March 11 at his home and asked him three questions. He did not reply clearly and I therefore visited him again at eight o'clock of the same day and repeated my questions. First, how did he visualize independent Slovak life after all constitutional links to Prague were ended? He evaded a clear answer. He denied my second question as to whether he as the newly appointed prime minister could guarantee my personal freedom. In reply to my third question, whether I should accompany him to the government office, he replied that I should return to my present hideout, which I naturally did not do, returning instead to my Guardists. It became clear to me that I was no longer in the proper place as political chief of staff of the Hlinka Guards under the present Prague-appointed prime minister Karol Sidor. I therefore called Karol Sidor at midnight asking him to release me from my position and from my oath, since my Slovak conscience no longer allowed me to serve a government that rested on nothing but the bayonets of Czech gendarmes. Karol Sidor did not accept my resignation, did not release me from my oath, and tried to postpone everything until today, Monday. Events of last night show clearly, however, why I was to wait until Monday. Yesterday, Sunday, at six o'clock in the morning I went to the government office for the last time in order to speak to Sidor. He was surrounded by a group of opportunistic Freemasons. I nevertheless made my way to him and said: "Karol, what you are doing is bad and a national disaster." That is how Karol Sidor and I parted ways. He is at this moment prime minister by the grace of the gentlemen of Prague and deals with Czech generals, while I am a Guardist, persecuted by the Czech police, who has remained faithful to Andrej Hlinka's great order of January 13, l938, at Zilina when he said, "Goodbye, Prague." The coming days will show who did the right thing for Slovakia and for Christianity, the present prime minister Karol Sidor, or the Guardist Karol Murgas.

Fellow Guardists! The hour has come; Slovak history has reached the crossroads. New life, freedom, and independence will follow. The great savior of national Europe, Adolf Hitler, holds his protecting hand over us; and if we can show that we are willing to live and die for freedom, the future is ours.

Fellow Guardists! Commanders! Comrades in arms! In this decisive hour I call out to you the burning words linking us in life and death: *Na straz!*

Sources: Handakten Seyss-Inquart. *Tu rissky,* pp. 53-56. Petreas, *Die Slowakei im Umbruch,* pp. 171-174. *Voelkischer Beobachter,* Vienna edition, March 14, 1939, p. 5.

Psychologically speaking, Murgas' words resemble those spoken on the previous days by Durcansky in that both men feel on the defensive about speaking to their fellow countrymen from abroad. They rationalize their position by showing the risks they have taken to escape, the need for their making their way to Vienna, etc. Whether their arguments were acceptable to the rank and file of their followers, not to speak of the average Slovak, is hard to determine.   Another similarity between Murgas' broadcast and the others beamed to Bratislava in this period lies in the attempt to make the Slovak loyalist element appear to be a small minority of the people. While the Vienna broadcast of March 11, 1300 hours, equated Slovak loyalists with a "group siding with Czechs and Jews," Murgas calls the armed forces of the Czechoslovak state who had taken over control of Slovakia following the dismissal of the Tiso government "terrorists."

As in the case of the Durcansky speech of the preceding day interesting insights result from a comparison of the official German texts with what Murgas actually said. The important difference lies in the second to last paragraph with its reference to Adolf Hitler's protecting hand over Slovakia, which was widely noted by all who heard the broadcast. Yet it is nowhere to be found in German official texts. The most likely reason for this again is that Germany did not want to be accused of intervening in Slovak affairs, or of prodding Slovaks to secede from Prague as indeed she was doing with all the political skill at her command.

It is of some significance that Sidor protested the Murgas broadcast to Seyss-Inquart and that the latter had the protest answered by one of the members of his staff. Seyss-Inquart's telephoned reply stated that he had received Sidor's protest rather late and that he was unable to stop the daily (Slovak) broadcasts of Radio Vienna. Anyway, he went on, Radio Vienna was supporting Sidor's policies, and it was Sidor who had deviated from them of late. Nevertheless, Seyss-Inquart was willing to meet Sidor that same afternoon at Engerau to discuss the Vienna radio issue.[16] Sidor declined this invitation and clarified that he had not intended that the Slovak broadcasts from Vienna be stopped, only that they not be used by members of the Hlinka Guards for incitement against their commander-in-chief.[17]

In other words, by the afternoon of March 13, when this exchange of messages took place, each man was not yet willing to break off relations with the other completely. Seyss-Inquart hoped to turn the discussion about the Vienna broadcasts into a last-minute attempt to change Sidor's mind on the issue of Slovak independence. Sidor politely refused Seyss-Inquart's suggestion for a meeting and referred to the fact that the entire issue was now being discussed at the highest level.[18] Tiso left for Berlin at noon of March 13 after having informed Sidor and the other leading Slovak political figures that Hitler had called him there for a conference.)

The question of Seyss-Inquart's control over the Vienna Slovak broadcasts is discussed in Chapter II.

In addition to its other importance, the Murgas speech affords valuable insight into German censorship of the Vienna Slovak language broadcasts. The daily journal kept in Seyss-Inquart's office contains an entry made at 0740 hours on March 13 to the effect that Seyss- Inquart's first assistant, Franz Hammerschmid, was specifically asked to carefully check Murgas' speech before it was delivered.[19]

Slovak language broadcast from Vienna, March 13, 1939, 1300 hours.

Tonight we received the following reports from Bratislava.

In its program of last night Radio Bratislava made a futile attempt to cast doubt on the reliability of the Slovak programs of Radio Vienna. Our brethren beneath the Tatra Mountains know very well whom they can trust and who has let them down once before in times of crisis. We remind them of the beautiful speeches which Radio Bratislava broadcast in the critical September days on orders from Prague. At that time, too, it was maintained that all was well and that the Slovak people were happy to walk hand in hand with the Czechs toward an abyss. The Slovak people realized very well where the truth was spoken; it was on Radio Vienna, since only Vienna was in a position to speak frankly and without the interference and control of Prague.

Today the situation is similar. Today also Prague has Slovakia under her control. Today also bayonets, armored cars, and machine guns are the physical means of applying pressure on the much-tried Slovak people. It does not improve the situation when the Bratislava radio says beautiful things and promises us full autonomy. Those promises have been made a thousand times already and have been broken a thousand times. That is one experience the Slovak people have learned to accept as a fact in the course of the last, sad twenty years.

What kind of independence and freedom is it when renowned leaders of our people languish in prison, when victims of Czech terrorism are carried to their graves, when the entire nation is in arms against its oppressors who are making a last frantic effort to maintain their rule. What kind of freedom is it when the radio is forced to kowtow to Prague, when the newspapers are censored which was rare even in the worst time of the Benes era loathsome though that was to Slovakia. What kind of freedom is it when well-known leaders of our people must hide or flee abroad to escape the terrorist measures of the Czech military. It is a condition unworthy of the Slovak people, a condition the Slovak people cannot and will not tolerate. Countless letters from Slovakia thank the Slovaks in Vienna for the Slovak broadcasts from Radio Vienna. These letters are the best proof that we are speaking from the heart of the Slovak people to the heart of our Slovak fellow countrmen.

And is it not obvious that Radio Prague and Radio Brno told the same story in their night broadcasts as did the nominally free Radio Bratislava? We are told that Radio Bratislava is in the hands of the Hlinka Guards. Do the Slovak people know that all the technical equipment of Radio Bratislava is controlled by heavily armed Czechs? If a single word against Prague's centralism were to be broadcast, that would be the end of the so-called freedom of Radio Bratislava.

No, the times of native credulity are gone forever. The game that Prague is playing against the true freedom of the Slovak people and against long-awaited Slovak independence has been discovered. Prague's reputation for truthfulness has been thoroughly discredited by the ordeal of the last twenty years.

Long live free Slovakia!

Speech of Rudolf Vavra, March 13, 1939, 1400 hours.[20]

As leader of the Slovaks in Germany I am addressing myself to all Slovaks who were deprived of their livelihood by the Czech invasion and who were forced to go abroad to avoid starvation. In the last few days the Czech Hussites[21] invaded our beloved Slovakia with tanks and machine guns in order to drown the steadily growing longing for an independent Slovakia in the blood of our best sons. The Slovaks abroad have set their heart on Slovak independence; they know that our starving brethren can only return home when 350,000 Czechs and Jews leave Slovakia. Therefore do not believe those who are in the pay of the Czechs. We want only what all Slovaks want Work and bread not through the grace of Czech overlords but through the free will and strength of our people.

It is intolerable that only Czechs and Jews lead the good life in Slovakia. Slovaks, however, can prosper only at the price of betraying their own people. And all Slovaks who had merely been able to settle on sufferance in the historic lands have now been expelled from them. They work in France or in Belgium for starvation wages, or they wander from country to country without employment. We have done nothing but constantly remind you of these truths. Let Mr. Cavojsky answer our question of how many Czechs and Jews have left Slovakia since October 6 as a result of his activity, and why it is that he was unable to find work for a single Slovak living abroad?[2] It was he who tried to get the Czech military authorities to arrest those loyal Slovaks abroad who had refused last September to fire on Germans at the whim of Mr. Benes. Furthermore, why has Mr. Cavojsky not drawn the consequences and why has he not made his exit from public life as did Mr. Benes? Did he not back Benes in his newspapers and praise his policies to the very end? By these actions he helped to provoke a catastrophic war which, had it come, would have sacrificed the Slovak nation for Judaeo-Bolshevik interests. Why do the Czechs allow Messrs. Cavojsky, Teplansky, and similar troublemakers to speak on Radio Bratislava, and why are Mach, Tuka, Murgas, Kirschbaum, etc. not allowed to do so?

We address ourselves to you Slovaks abroad. The hour is near. Slovakia is approaching independence. The traditional Slovak broadcasts from Vienna will then be taken over by Radio Bratislava which will at last be truly Slovak, and Slovaks abroad will then be able to return to their beloved homeland.

Slovak brethren, I believe that we have accomplished honestly and unselfishly our mission of serving as a bond between Slovakia and Germany, while at the same time helping achieve the duty of every self-confident nation, namely the independence of the Slovak people.

May the Lord help us in our struggle! Victory is ours!

We have just received word that the executive committee of the Hlinka Party has decided at its meeting today to send two emissaries to Berlin. They are Monsignore Dr. Josef Tiso and deputy Stefan Danihel. Both crossed the Slovak border at Petrzalka at noon.

Sources: Documents of the SD-Leitabschnitt Vienna. *News Chronicle,* London, March 14, 1939. For reference to Vavra's speech see Petreas, *Die Slowakei im Umbruch,* p. 174.

Two propagandistic tendencies are noteworthy in Vavra's speech. The first is the continuation of the earlier noted tendency of German and pro-German Slovak propagandists to list their opponents as Czechs and Jews. By doing so they are using a standard propaganda device to create the impression that the Slovak people as such were solidly behind their extremist stand on separatism, and that anyone opposing it could only be a Czech or a Jew.

The other tendency is to make economic motivations, which forced the large bulk of Slovak emigrants to leave their country, appear identical with political motivations of a few anti-Czech emigrants including Vavra himself.

A note of unintentional irony is supplied by Vavra's promise that once independence is achieved, the Vienna Slovak broadcasts would no longer be needed. In actual fact the Slovak broadcasts from Vienna continued long after the creation of an independent Slovak state, and there were many instances when the new Slovak government resented their interference in Slovak affairs.

Speech by Viliam Kovar, March 13, 1939, 1600 hours.[23]

Dear Guardist-Academicians!

Only a very short time separates us from the fulfillment of our national aspiration—the creation of an independent Slovakia. Academicians! You have always been close to the main artery of Slovak life. Since the World War you have been guardians of Slovak freedom against all enemies. You have not feared any sacrifice in this struggle. You have organized demonstrations in Trencianske Teplice, Nitra,[24] under the brave slogan "Slovakia for the Slovaks", and you dealt the mortal blow to the old regime which denied Slovak national rights. Through your demonstrations you have mobilized all of Slovakia. The celebrations in Bratislava of the Pittsburgh Agreement anniversary were a clear signal that the victory of Slovak truth could not be delayed or stopped.[25] The last order of our immortal leader Andrej Hlinka was addressed to we academicians. The achievement of Slovak autonomy was partly your work, but you remained at your posts even longer. In your journal *Nastup* you fought fearlessly for a completely independent Slovakia. This battle, too, is nearing its end.

I do not need to give you counsel or orders. Maintain the posture you have always maintained, especially during these last few days when Slovak freedom has been at stake. You have given proof of the fact that you are brave and fearless fighters, and this fearlessness, courage, and imperturbability will once again determine our complete Slovak victory. *Na straz!*

Sources: Documents of the SD-Leitabschnitt Vienna. Kovar, "Notizen aus den Maerztagen 1939," pp. 26, 27. For reference to Kovar's speech see *News Chronicle,* London, March 14, 1939.

Following the speech of Viliam Kovar there was at least one further Slovak language program at 1815 hours. It consisted of a letter from a group of listeners favoring Slovak independence. This broadcast has been omitted from the series because of its minor importance.

Later in the same evening of March 13 (probably at 2130 hours) another speech by Karol Murgas[26] was broadcast. It has also been omitted, partly because the only text the author has been able to locate is merely that of a draft taken down by Viliam Kovar on dictation from Karol Murgas and partly because the content of the speech consists mostly of personal recriminations between Murgas and his successor as the Hlinka Guards' chief of staff, Pavel Carnogursky, who had attacked Murgas earlier in the evening on Radio Bratislava.

More interesting than the contents of the Murgas speech of that evening, however, are the circumstances surrounding it. For one thing we know on German authority that the initiative for Murgas' speech came from Dr. Walter Stahlecker, a leading police official on Seyss-Inquart's staff. Once again we note the close involvement of the Germans with what was purported to be an expression of Slovak public opinion.[27] A further circumstance of some importance is that the speech may have been read for Murgas by the announcer of the Slovak broadcasts Ludovit Mutnansky in order to create the impression that Murgas had returned to Bratislava.[28] Whether this ruse was used because it was felt that the listeners would have more confidence in a man who braved danger to return home in such critical hours, or because it was felt that Murgas' presence at home would help rally the radical elements in the Hlinka Guards and would add to the woes of the Sidor government cannot be established with any certainty. We do know, however, that Murgas was in the Vienna studios while the speech was read and that shortly thereafter Seyss-Inquart paid the Slovak section of Radio Vienna the honor of a personal visit, thus giving an indication of the politcal importance the broadcasts had assumed at that moment.

After the climactic events of the preceeding days there came the Vienna station's triumphal announcement of Slovak independence on March 14, 1939. The two following broadcasts of that day were read by Ludovit Mutnansky.
Slovak broadcast from Vienna, March 14, 1939, 1310 hours.

Slovaks of the entire world listen! We announce the most joyous Slovak news. Today at twelve o'clock noon the independent Slovak state was proclaimed. "Long live the eternal Slovak spirit. Thunder and Hell have fought it in vain."[29]

Long live the Slovak people! Long live the Slovak state!
Slovak broadcast from Vienna, March 14, 1939, 1400 hours.

Ring Slovak bells! Announce the joyous news of the birth of the Slovak state! At this happy moment when the heart of every Slovak man and woman is full of joy, we thank those men who made it possible for us to say as of 1213 hours today that we have an independent Slovak state. The Slovak people have their state.

Our gratitude at this moment goes out to the cemetery of Ruzomberok where our dear, immortal leader Andrej Hlinka is buried.

Sleep in peace, dear father. The Slovak people are free and independent and will remain so. In the Slovak diet a marble tablet will be inscribed for eternal memory: "To Andrej Hlinka for meritorious services to the Slovak people and state."

In this joyous hour Slovaks think with grateful and sincere love of Adolf Hitler, the great leader of our friends and neighbors. The name Adolf Hitler means much to our Slovak people, and were it not for his approval there would be no Slovak state.

Ring Slovak bells! Announce the joyous news of the birth of the Slovak state, the state of a small but eternally young and honest people.

Men and women of Slovakia! Guardists!

From September 15, 1938, until today, day by day, week by week, month by month, we fought our battle on the airwaves for Slovak rights and freedom. We walked a straight, uncompromising path. We did not listen to false and hypocritical opinions but followed the direction of our Slovak heart, conscience, and reason.

Our work and our struggle were hard, but honest and manly. Today we can exclaim with joy and in good conscience that we have won after all. Our slogan is: "To turn back is impossible; we must march forward."

When today world history and the Slovak people register this important event, it will be due also to a small and modest extent to Radio Vienna.

We fought among other things for the right of Slovaks to return to their own country from which they had been driven by an unwanted fate. We shall continue the work we have begun.

Brothers and sisters, we are starting to build our independent Slovak state. We are starting to build our own home. We shall be united, we shall be honest, and we shall be grateful to those who made this victory possible for us.

We send our thanks to all those honest fighters who served the cause of Slovak independence.

We cordially call out to all Slovaks: *Na straz!*

Sources: Tu rissky, pp. 57, 58. *Slovenska Revolucia,* pp. 89-91.

Remarkable about this broadcast is the agility with which Mutnansky stresses Hitler's part in making Slovak independence possible, yet maintains the myth that all Hitler had to do to bring this about was to give it his approval. We know that his role was far greater and more direct than that, and Mutnansky unwittingly brings out one of the many actions taken by Hitler to subvert a united Czechoslovakia when he stresses the role of the Vienna radio station in the events leading to March 14, 1939.

[1]The use of this term for the radio activity between March 10 and March 14, 1939 is based on Hubert Ripka, *Munich: Before and After* (London: Victor Gollancz, 1939), p. 368, and on Hoensch, *Die Slowakei,* p. 273, footnote 17.

[2]Pavel Teplansky was Slovak minister of economics and finance from October 7, 1938 to January 19, 1939, and minister of finance from January 20 to March 11, 1939.

[3]Reference to the Munich crisis of September 1938.

[4]General Bedrich Homola, commander in central Slovakia, had declared martial law on March 9, 1939.

[5]Dates on which the Slovak diet was elected and then voted unanimously to accept the Tiso government's program, respectively.

[6]Karol Sidor was Slovak minister of state in the Czechoslovak central government, deputy premier of the Czechoslovak central government December 1, 1938, to March 14, 1939, and prime minister of Slovakia March 11 to 14, 1939.

[7]Hlinka Guard salute, meaning literally: Be on guard. It later became the official Slovak state salute comparable to the German *Heil Hitler.*

[8]Roennefarth, *Die Sudetenkrise,* p. 733.

[9]Teletype no. 785 of March 11, 1939, 0136 hours, from Seyss- Inquart to Minister Schmidt, Foreign Office, Berlin. Handakten Seyss-Inquart.

[10]Sources used in this commentary on the broadcast include the following: *Documents on British Foreign Policy,* vol. IV, nos. 208 & 212. Durica, *La Slovacchia e le sue Relazioni Politiche,* p. 172. *French Yellow Book,* p. 78. Hoensch, *Die Slowakei,* p. 273, R. G. D. Laffan, *Survey of International Affairs,* 1938, vol. III (London: Oxford University Press, 1953), p.228. Petreas, *Die Slowakei im Umbruch,* p. 159. Hubert Ripka, *Munich: Before and After* (London: Victor Gollancz, 1939), p. 367. *Grenzbote,* March 11, 1939. *The New York Times,* March 11, 1939.

[11]Reference to Sidor's speech of March 11, 0015 hours, see comment on Durcansky speech of March 10.

[12]Reference to the Slovak autonomy law passed in November 1938.

[13]Sources used in this commentary include the following: *Documents on British Foreign Policy,* vol.IV, no. 215; Hoensch, *Die Slowakei,* pp. 266, 283.

[14]The exact hour of the broadcast is not known to the author but it was close to the noon hour of March 13.

[15]Martin Sokol was president of the Slovak diet; Julius Stano was vice president of the Slovak diet; and Peter Zatko was appointed minister of economics on March 11, 1939. Sokol and Stano were also appointed to cabinent offices (ministers of interior and of transportation respectively) on March 11, 1939.

[16]Engerau (Slovak name Petrzalka), on the south bank of the Danube facing Bratislava, was turned over to Germany after the Munich Agreement.

[17]Sidor's version of this incident is taken from Sidor, *Ako vznikol "Slovensky*

Stat," p. 2l. The German version is from Handakten Seyss-Inquart, Journal of March 13, 1939, entry under 1400 hours.

[18]The movement of negotiations to the highest level was equally true on the German side where Seyss-Inquart and Buerckel were shunted aside by Berlin after March ll, having first been subjected to criticism by Hitler's roving ambassador Wilhelm Keppler for their failure to bring the question of Slovak independence to a successful conclusion.

[19]Handakten Seyss-Inquart, Journal of March 12-13, 1939, entry under 0740 hours of March 13. Sources used in this commentary include the following: Pierre Buk, *La Tragedie Tchecoslovaque* (Paris: Editions du Sagittaire, 1939), p. 186, (Murgas's speech mistakenly attributed to Durcansky). John B. Whitton and John H. Herz, "Radio in Internatinal Politics," *Propaganda by Shortwave* (Princeton: Princeton University Press, 1942), p. 38. Hoensch, *Die Slowakei,* p. 266. Roennefarth, *Die Sudetenkrise,* p. 733. *News Chronicle,* London, March 14, 1939.

[20]Vavra was the leading spokesman of the pro-German Slovaks in Vienna and after Slovakia became independent was made the Slovak consul there.

[21]This is one of the favorite propaganda slogans used by Slovaks in exhorting their fellow countryment against the Czechs. The derogatory term Hussite was designed to arouse fear and hate in staunchly Catholic Slovaks. The movement to which the term refers originated in the Czech part of the nation in the fifteenth century and is considered one of the forerunners of the Reformation. The element of fear aroused by the term is due to the fact that the Hussite movement spurred bloody peasant uprisings.

[22]Rudo Cavojsky was a Slovak People's Party deputy and the leading official of the Slovak Labor Union.

[23]Viliam Kovar was the leader of the student section of the Hlinka Guards.

[24]The Trencianske Teplice Convention of the Young Generation took place June 25 and 26, 1932, and the Nitra anniversary celebrations of 1100 years of Christianity in Central Europe were held on August 13, 1933.

[25]The Pittsburgh Agreement of May 30, 1918, was concluded between Czech and Slovak organizations in the United States to form a united state. Slovaks later felt that the Czechs had not lived up to the agreement's equal rights guarantee to both groups. The celebration referred to by Kovar took place on June 5, 1938, when a large throng, headed by Andrej Hlinka, greeted American Slovaks who were visiting Slovakia and who had brought the original of the agreement along.

[26]Kovar, "Notizen aus den Maerztagen 1939," pp. 28-30.

[27]Handakten Seyss-Inquart, Journal of March 13, 1939, entry under 1745 hours.

[28]*Ibid.,* entry under 1845 hours.

[29]Part of the Slovak national anthem.

Glossary

Benes, Eduard.
> Second president of Czechoslovakia. Resigned presidency on October 5, 1938, following the Munich Agreement and went into exile where he organized Czech resistance. Returned to his country after the end of the war and resumed presidency from which he resigned again in June 1948 after the Communist coup in Czechoslovakia. Died shortly thereafter.

Buerckel, Joseph.
> Responsible for the succesul reintegration of the Saar area into Germany in 1935, he was made Gauleiter of Austria after the Anschluss, in which capacity he participated actively in German pressure on Slovakia to declare her independence. Later he became Gauleiter of Moravia. Committed suicide in 1944.

Durcansky, Dr. Ferdinand.
> Minister of Justice, later minister of transport in the autonomous Slovak regime after October 6, 1938. He became foreign minister after Slovak independence but, though originally pro-German was removed from that position in July 1940 on German insistence. Died in Munich, West-Germany, March 1974.

Hacha, Emil.
> President of Czechoslovakia from November 30, 1938 to March 15, 1939.

Hlinka, Mgr. Andrej.
> Founder and leader of the Slovak People's Party until his death in August 1938.

Karmasin, Franz.
> Leader of German minority in Slovakia and representative of that group in the Slovak government. Presently residing in Munich, West Germany.

Kovar, Viliam.
> Leader of student section of Hlinka Guards in days preceding independence.

Mach, Alexander.
> (Sano). Propaganda chief of autonomous Slovakia and member of the pro-German wing of Slovak People's Party. After independence he was made interior minister. Tried in Czechoslovakia after the war, he was given a sentence of thirty years in prison and was paroled in 1968.

Masaryk, Thomas G.
> Founder and first president of Czechoslovakia, 1918-135. Died in 1937.

Muehlberger, Dr. Wolfgang.
>   (see biographical data in Chapter II). Deputy Director of South European broadcasts of Radio Vienna in 1938 and 1939. In this capacity Muehlberger was in charge of Radio Vienna's propaganda campaign against Slovakia.

Murgas, Karol.
>   Slovak People's Party journalist and leader of the political staff of the Hlinka Guards during autonomy period. Fell out with Sidor in crisis preceding independence.

Mutnansky, Ludovit.S
>   (see biographical data in Chapter II). Slovak propagandist and author of most of the Vienna broadcasts to Slovakia between September 1938 and August 1939.

Ribbentrop, Joachim von.
>   German foreign minister from February 1938 until the end of the Third Reich. Tried, convicted, and hanged at Nuremberg, October 1946.

Seyss-Inquart, Dr. Arthur.
>   Briefly cabinet member in pre-Anschluss Austria, after Anschluss for a short time Austrian chancellor, then Reichsstatthalter of Austria. It was in this capacity that Seyss-Inquart was entrusted by Hitler with the additional task of collecting information from (i.e., subverting) Slovakia. After Slovakia became independent Seyss-Inquart was considered for the post of German ambassador to that country, but this position was deemed too unimportant. He was made a Reichsminister without portfolio on May 1, 1939. After Poland was conquered later in the year, he briefly served as deputy to Hans Frank, the German governor of that country. In May 1940 he was made Reichskommissar for the Netherlands. For his activity in that position he was later tried and convicted at the Nuremberg trials and was hanged October 1946.

Sidor, Karol.
>   Leading member of the Slovak People's Party. First commander of the Hlinka Guards. Served as Slovak vice-premier of Czechoslovak central regime after Czech state adopted a federal regime in December 1938. Served as premier of Slovakia between March 11 and March 14, 1939. Was then appointed Slovak minister to the Vatican. Emigrated to Canada at war's end and died in Montreal in 1954.

Tiso, Mgr. Jozef.
>   Premier and later president of Slovakia. Tried by the Czechoslovak government between December 1946 and April 1947, he was executed April 18, 1947.

Teplansky, Pavel.
    Slovak minister of economics and finance, October 7, 1938- January 19, 1939; Minister of finance, January 20, 1939-March 11, 1939.
Tuka, Dr. Vojtech.
    Leading pro-German separatist statesman in Slovakia. Started as editor of People's Party newspaper; was tried and convicted of treason in 1929 and sentenced to fifteen years of prison. Released prematurely in 1937 but confined to the Plzen area, he was allowed to return to Slovakia in October 1938. After Slovak independence he became next to Tiso the leading figure and longtime premier of independent Slovakia. Tried by a Czechoslovak court and hanged in August 1946. Member of pro-German wing of Slovak People's Party.
Vavra, Rudolf.
    Leader of Nazi-oriented Vienna Slovaks. Became Slovak consul in Vienna after independence.

Chronology

General Background of Czech-Slovak Union

October 22, 1915, Cleveland Agreement and May 30, 1918, Pittsburgh Agreement: Agreements between Czechs and Slovaks in the United States to join in a common state at the end of World War I.
October 30, 1918, Declaration of St. Martin: Document setting forth views of a group of prominent Slovaks on postwar cooperation with Czechs.
Events of 1938-1939.

1938

Mar. 13	Germany annexes Austria.
May 30	Hitler issues directive to armed forces declaring that it is his "unalterable will to smash Czechoslovákia by military action in the near future."
June 18	Hitler finalizes his directive on Czechoslovakia and adds date of October 1 for beginning of operations.
June 22	Seyss-Inquart writes to Ribbentrop asking for information on plans for Czech language broadcasts.
Sept. 3	Start of Czech language broadcasts from Vienna.
Sept. 15	Start of Slovak broadcasts from Vienna.
Sept. 19	German Foreign Ofice orders German minority leader Kundt to ask Slovaks to raise their autonomy demands the following day.
Sept. 26	Hitler speaks at Sportpalast, Berlin, mentioning Slovaks' desire to go their own peaceful way and avoid Czech adventures.
Sept. 29	Vienna Slovaks meet and form "Free Slovak Legion."
Oct. 5	President Benes resigns.
Oct. 6	Zilina Agreement of Slovak parties is made declaring autonomy. Jozef Tiso becomes head of Slovak autonomous government.
Oct. 21	Hitler issues directive to armed forces to be prepared to smash remainder of Czech state.
Oct. 23	Tuka, freed from house arrest in Plzen, returns to Slovakia.
Nov. 1	Slovak-Polish border settlement is made. Slovakia cedes approximately 167 square kilometers and 8,000 inhabitants. Sir Basil Newton, British minister in Prague, reports to Foreign Office that the Germans are broadcasting pro-independence propaganda to Slovakia.
Nov. 2	Vienna Award settles Czechoslovak-Hungarian border dispute by awarding approximately 10,000 square kilometers and 850,000 inhabitants of Slovakia to Hungary. Also parts of easternmost Czechoslovak province of Ruthenia awarded to Hungary.

Nov. 17	Bill for Slovak autonomy introduced in Prague parliament.
Nov. 19	Prague lower house passes Slovak autonomy bill.
Nov. 22	Prague upper house passes Slovak autonomy bill.
Nov. 30	Emil Hacha elected president of Czechoslovakia.
Dec. 1	President Hacha formally appoints Slovak government.
Dec. 6	Tuka returns to Bratislava.
Dec. 9	Tuka, speaking in Bratislava, demands Slovak independence.
Dec. 18	Elections for Slovak diet held.
1939	
Jan. 18	Slovak diet is opened.
Feb. 5	Slovak Propaganda Chief Mach, speaking at Risnovce, demands independence.
Feb. 12	Vienna Slovaks form Andrej Hlinka League.
Feb. 19	Sidor and Mach address Andrej Hlinka League in Vienna.
Feb. 21	Slovak government declaration of its program omits mention of Czechoslovak state.
Feb. 23	Unanimous approval of government declaration is given by Slovak diet.
Mar. 7	Seyss-Inquart visits Tiso and urges him to demand independnce.
Mar. 9	President Hacha dismisses Tiso government.
Mar. 10	Durcansky sends premature appeal for Hitler's intervention. Durcansky broadcasts to Slovakia from Vienna.
Mar. 11	Hacha appoints Karol Sidor premier of Slovakia. Seyss-Inquart visits Sidor and urges him to demand independence.
Mar. 12	Tiso reports German threat to occupy Bratislava unless he visits Hitler.
Mar. 13	Hitler receives Tiso and Durcansky. Murgas broadcasts from Vienna.
Mar. 14	Slovak diet meets, accepts Sidor's resignation and declares independence.
Mar. 15	Hitler receives President Hacha, who surrenders his country to Hitler. German troops enter Bohemia, Moravia, and western part of Slovakia.
Mar. 16	Slovakia asks Germany for protective alliance.
Mar. 23	Slovak-German protection treaty is signed.

Bibliography

Primary Sources

Akten zur deutschen auswaertigen Politik, 1918-1945,series D,IV. Baden-Baden: Imprimierie Nationale, 1950-1958. Abbrev. ADAP.

Archives of Sound Documents of the Czechoslovak Radio. Sound documents in text. Sound Documents of the Czechoslovak Radio. Sound documents in text. Series 2, Vol. 2: *Czech and Slovak Broadcasts from Vienna, September 1938, March 1939.* Unpublished manuscript. *Note:* This manuscript was made available to the author by courtesy of the Czechoslovak Radio after the completion of the manuscript for this book. Some minor differences from texts reported in the other sources used were found but none of them were of sufficient importance to warrant a major revision of the manuscript.

Baynes, Norman H. *The Speeches of Adolf Hitler,* vol. II. London: Oxford University Press, 1942.

Department of State Special Interrogation Mission to Germany, 1945-46. Microfilm M-679, National Archives, Washington, D.C.

Documents of the SD-Leitabschnitt Vienna. Microfilm T-175, serial 514, roll 514. National Archives, Washington, D.C.

Documents on British Foreign Policy, 3rd series, vols.III and IV. London: His Majesty's Stationery Office. 1950-51.

Documents on German Foreign Policy, series D, vol. IV. Washington, D.C.: U.S. Government Printing Office, 1951.

Handakten Seyss-Inquart, Bundesarchiv, Coblenz.

Muehlberger, Wolfgang. *Arbeits- und Organisationsbericht ueber die tschechischen, slowakischen und ukrainischen Relationen des Reichssenders Wien.* Handakten Seyss-Inquart, Bundesarchiv, Coblenz.

Muehlberger, Wolfgang. *Zur politischen Entwicklung in der Slowakei.* Microfilm T-120, serial 2003, roll 1141, frames 442381-442384. National Archives, Washington D.C.

Mutnansky, Ludovit. *Tu rissky vysielac Vieden.* Vienna: Julius Lichtner, 1939.

Mutnansky, Ludovit. *Slovenska Revolucia na Vlnach Eteru.* Bratislava: Nakladom vlastnym, 1942.

Political Archives, Bonn Foreign Office. Microfilm T-120, serial 2003, roll 1141, National Archives, Washington, D.C.

Political Archives, Bonn Foreign Office. "Durchfuehrung des Muenchener Abkommens." File pol. IV. Microfilm.

The French Yellow Book. New York: Reynal & Hitchcock, 1940.

Trial of the Major War Criminals. Nuremberg, Germany, 1947. Abbrev. IMT.

Secondary Sources
Books

Buk, Pierre. *La Tragedie Tchecoslovaque*. Paris: Editions du Sagittaire, 1939.

Chreno, Jozef. *Maly Slovnik Slovenskeho Statu*. Bratislava, 1965.

Davidson, Eugene. *The Trial of the Germans*. New York: MacMillan, 1966.

Durica, Milan Stanislao. *La Slovacchia e le sue Relazioni Politiche con la Germania 1938-1945*. Padua: Marsilio Editor: 1964.

Hagemann, Walter. *Publizistik im Dritten Reich*. Hamburg: Hansischer Gildenverlag, 1948.

Hagen, Walter (Wilhelm Hoettl). *Die geheime Front*. Linz: Nibelungen Verlag, 1950.

Henderson, Alexander. *Eyewitness in Czechoslovakia*. London: George G. Harrap & Co., 1939.

Hoensch, Joerg K. *Die Slowakei und Hitlers Ostpolitik*. Cologne, Graz: Boehlau Verlag, 1965.

Kennan, George F. *From Prague after Munich* Princeton: Princeton University Press, 1968.

Kovar, Viliam. "Notizen aus den Maerztagen 1939 'als die Freiheit geboren wurde.'" Unpublished manuscript.

Laffan, R.G.D. *Survey of International Affairs, 1938*. vol.III. London: Oxford University Press, 1953.

Lettrich, Jozef. *History of Modern Slovakia*. New York: Frederick A. Praeger, 1955.

Loewenheim, Francis L. *Peace or Appeasement?* Boston: Houghton Mifflin Co., 1965.

Lukacs, John A. *The Great Powers and Eastern Europe*. New York: American Book Co., 1953.

Oddo, Gilbert L. *Slovakia and its People*. New York: Speller, 1960.

Petreas, Johann Oskar. *Die Slowakei im Umbruch*. Turcianske St. Martin: Kompas, 1941.

Roennefarth, Helmuth K.G. *Die Sudetenkrise in der Internationalen Politik*. Wiesbaden: Franz Steiner Verlag GMBH, 1961.

Ripka, Hubert. *Munich: Before and After*. London: Victor Gollancz, 1939.

Schulthess, *Europaeischer Geschichtskalender 1939*. Munich: C.H. Beck'sche Verlagsbuchhandlung, 1940.

Seton-Watson, R.W. *From Munich to Danzig*. London: Methuen & Co. Ltd., 1939.

Sidor, Karol. *Ako vznikol "Slovensky Stat."* Bratislava: Vydalo Poverenictvo pre informacie, 1945.

Stanek, Imrich. *Zrada a Pad*. Prague: Statni nakladatelstvi Politicke Literatury, 1958.

Wheeler-Bennett, John W. *Munich, Prologue to Tragedy*. New York: Viking Press, 1964.

Zeman, Z.A.B. *Nazi Propaganda*. London: Oxford University Press, 1964.

Articles

Jelinek, Yeshayahu. "Bohemia-Moravia, Slovakia and the Third Reich during the Second World War." *East European Quarterly,* vol. 3, no. 2 (June 1969), pp. 229-239.

Stiehler, Wilhelm. "Tu Rissky Vysielac Vieden." *Rundpost,* June 17, 1939.

Vnuk, Frantisek. "Slovakia's Six Eventful Months October 1938- March 1939." *Slovak Studies,* vol. 4 (1964), pp. 7-164.

Weir, Edgar. "Radio Propaganda the New Weapon of War." *News Chronicle,* March 14, 1939.

Whitton, John B. and Herz, John H. "Radio in International Politics." In *Propaganda by Short Wave,* edited by Harwood L. Childs and John B. Whitton. Princeton: Princeton University Press, 1942.

Newspapers

Daily Telegraph and Morning Post, London
*Grenzbote,*Bratislava
Neue Freie Presse, Vienna
Neues Wiener Tagblatt, Vienna
News Chronicle, London
The New York Times
Voelkischer Beobachter, Vienna edition

Books used in connection with Talmudic Passages

Babylonian Talmud (Hebrew edition). Jerusalem: El Hamekorot Ltd., 1958-1963.

Der Babylonische Talmud (German edition). Edited by Lazarus Goldschmidt. Berlin: S. Calvary & Co., 1903.

Ecker, Jacob. *Der "Judenspiegel."* Paderborn: Bonifacius Druckerei, 1884.

Eisenmenger, Johann Andreas. *Entdecktes Judenthum.* Koenigsberg, 1711.

INDEX